EXPLORING PAST LIVES

to Heal the Present

EXPLORING PAST LIVES

to Heal the Present

Debbie Johnson

ECKANKAR
Minneapolis

Exploring Past Lives to Heal the Present

Edited by Joan Klemp, Anthony Moore, and Mary Carroll Moore

Author photo by Glamour Shots

Publisher's Cataloging-in-Publication
(Provided by Quality Books, Inc.)

Johnson, Debbie.
    Exploring past lives to heal the present / Debbie Johnson.
    p. cm.
    Includes bibliographical references.
    LCCN: 2004100524
    ISBN: 1-57043-198-1

    1. Eckankar (Organization) 2. Reincarnation.
3. Spiritual healing. I. Title.

BP605.E3J64 2004   299'.93
                            QBI33-1791

Contents

Acknowledgments

Many people contributed to this book and encouraged me as I moved forward, like a snail at times, through many edits. Thank you so much for all of your help and support.

Kimberly Young was especially positive and supportive, and to her I extend special gratitude. Also I thank Marjorie Klemp for the historical research she shared with me.

I am most grateful for the time taken by all the people who allowed me to interview them and were willing to answer tough questions to make richer stories.

For editing that brought this book to the point of being accepted for publishing, thank you to Adrian McBride for his tremendous help and to Dick Ridington for his insights and comments.

To the staff at Eckankar who hone every project until it sings and shines with the Light and Sound of God, thank you for your loving dedication.

And for his unending patience, guidance, and love which made this book possible, I thank the Mahanta, my constant inner companion, spiritual teacher, and angel of the highest order.

Foreword

*P*anic, fear, and anxiety gripped me as I stood in my kitchen. What nonsense this was! I was paralyzed by fear every time I prepared food for company. There was no problem when I cooked just for myself. Why was I so frightened of cooking for guests?

I had to know.

So I tried one of the exercises I give in this book. From a past-life recall that came, I realized I got this fear in another life—a lifetime when I was beheaded for a meal that made the king unhappy.

Now it all made sense!

Over time, this insight helped heal the panic, fear, and anxiety about cooking for others. The healing and awareness of lessons from that life—and other lives—came from exercises learned in years of study and spiritual practice.

I have always been interested in past lives. When I was eight I remember thinking, *I must have lived before!* I had just watched a movie filmed in England, and I began thinking in an English accent. My parents had never spoken of reincarnation. I had never heard of it before, yet I knew it existed. And I knew I had been English in a previous life. But I never talked about my perceptions, feeling I wouldn't be understood.

When I was thirteen, my best friend told me about the book *The Search for Bridey Murphy* by Morey Bernstein.[1]

Bernstein sought to prove the theory of reincarnation by validating patients' memories with research. I was thrilled at the possibilities of reincarnation being real. After reading that book, I read a book by Joan Grant on reincarnation. This was in the 1960s. Who on earth could I talk to about this fascinating subject? I just knew past lives were real, but I didn't dare talk about them.

Years went by. Finally I found others who believed what I did. And some even remembered a few of their own past lives.

What a relief! I wasn't alone.

Many people have the same questions about past lives I did:

- What is love at first sight, and why does it happen so often?
- What's behind the mystery of child prodigies?
- How can one place seem so strange and another so familiar?
- Why are some people born physically challenged and others able bodied?

Eastern and Western religions alike have addressed these questions in theories of reincarnation and karma. The New Testament speaks of reincarnation in Luke 9:8, referring to one of the old prophets, Elias, having "risen" again as John.[2] There's also John 3:13: "No man hath ascended up to heaven, but he that came down from heaven."[3]

I found some great information in theology and spiritual writings on past lives, but at first I wasn't that interested in exploring my own.

Not until I discovered I could explore my past lives to heal my present life!

Learning about my past lives, using the same methods I share in this book, helped me heal a broken heart, discover the cause of financial problems, find a way to improve relationships, and more.

The method is simple and direct, inspired by a very ancient spiritual teaching streamlined for modern times. It's called Eckankar, Religion of the Light and Sound of God.

Most of the ideas and tools in this book come from the study of Eckankar and the writings of its spiritual leader, Harold Klemp. He is a world-renowned expert on the subject of Soul Travel, dreams, reincarnation, and other spiritual topics. He describes many accounts of past lives and gives spiritual insights on reincarnation throughout his published works. I refer to his writings often. Because of his experience and spiritual awareness, he is the greatest expert on past lives I know of.

For this book, I also interviewed many people who've had insights into past lives that were affecting them in this one. I give their stories, as close as possible, in their own words. However, all names and some unrelated circumstances have been changed to protect their privacy. The most important benefit they gave for understanding their past lives was to become more aware of who they really are.

Their stories offer examples of how this awareness can help us heal now and move beyond our present understanding into a more spiritual view of life

When exploring their past lives, the people I interviewed did not use hypnosis, trance, or other psychic methods. Nor did I. Such methods may pull us into negative areas we do not need or want to get into. Also, those methods are unnecessary when using simple spiritual or dream techniques like those you'll find in this book. These techniques are quite useful if you wish to gain greater spiritual awareness—consciously—to move toward a higher level of self-mastery.

Anyone can explore past lives very easily, consciously, and in full self-control. All it takes is a strong desire to discover what might be holding you back in this life, a little effort, and a genuine trust in God for guidance.

Perhaps you will catch a glimpse, or more, of one of your own past lives with the exercises in this book.

They use your waking awareness as well as your dreams. The wonderful thing is, you don't have to remember a specific lifetime for it to help you heal now! Just by using the exercises, you will gain whatever insights you need, whether or not you remember all the details of a specific past life.

In these pages you'll be given many tools to help you. You'll find chapters with true stories about healing relationships, health problems, finances, and more. If you have children, you'll find information that may help you understand them better.

You'll read about spiritual principles relating to past lives, like the nature of Soul, karma, and divine love. You'll be able to choose from different "Exploration Exercises" to learn to remember your past lives and work through past-life issues. And finally, in the last chapter, you'll find advanced spiritual tools to go beyond reincarnation and karma.

I was interested in past lives because, like the people I interviewed, I wanted to know who I really was and why I was here.

Through my studies in Eckankar, I now know we have lived lifetime after lifetime. In these lower worlds, we take on bodies like clothing, to experiment with different thoughts, emotions, and actions. Yet we are none of these things. In time the realization comes that we are something much greater.

We are Soul, the essence of God's love. And we are here to learn to express that love under every circumstance and condition.

This is how you can take charge of your life.

1
Waking Up to Past Lives

*All of us have lived before. You've had
some very good experiences and some very bad
experiences. When you come into this life,
certain of those experiences are going to be
highlighted for you because this is what you
need to work out.*

— Harold Klemp, *The Slow Burning Love of God,*
Mahanta Transcripts, Book 13[1]

*M*artha couldn't understand why she always
felt like an employee in her own home. Her
husband seemed to treat her like she worked for him,
even when talking to her about the international
business that *she* owned! He gave her orders, not
suggestions.

What was going on?

Following an inner nudge, Martha decided to
look into the possibility of a past life with her husband. She used an exercise much like the first one
you'll find in this chapter. She asked for spiritual
guidance. Next she looked at the phrase "I feel like
an employee" and examined the emotions behind it.
Then she relaxed and freely let images come to mind.

The first thing that came to her was an image of being a wealthy woman living alone in a huge house. She was seated at a dressing table, brushing her long beautiful hair.

She looked further and saw that she had two employees, both very unhappy. They were a married couple who lived in a shack on the estate. They felt she treated them unfairly. She would not let them live in the big, empty house and paid them little. Martha saw that as the owner of the estate, she was also very condescending and disdainful of her hired help.

> The realization struck Martha that she was being treated by her husband in this life exactly the way she had treated her employees in the past life she remembered.

The realization struck Martha that she was being treated by her husband in this life exactly the way she had treated her employees in the past life she remembered. Relying on her spiritual guidance, she looked inwardly again and had a sense that the male employee was her present husband, and the wife was her present-life mother-in-law! As she thought more about it, Martha gained more insight into her relationship with her mother-in-law as well, who had the habit of telling Martha what to do in no uncertain terms.

It all fell into place like pieces of a difficult jigsaw puzzle. Now Martha knew what it felt like to be treated unfairly, and so she began to have more compassion for others in the same situation. Almost immediately, she noticed a change in herself—and even in her husband.

Why Remember Past Lives?

Past-life memories can bring healing to present situations that mystify everyone involved. For example, as in Martha's story, relationships may suffer from past-life problems that neither partner can understand. A person's health may not improve, even after lengthy treatment, due to a past-life transgression. Finances may flounder endlessly if a past-life debt is still being repaid. Extreme heights or enclosed spaces may frighten some people when a past-life death or tragedy occurred in similar circumstances.

Exploring past lives may help resolve these issues or bring about a greater spiritual understanding of them. Such awareness can bring us closer to the realization of who we really are and what we are here to accomplish.

WHO ARE YOU REALLY AND WHY ARE YOU HERE?

Are you an eternal being, as most religions profess?

Yes! You are Soul. You will never die, only your body will. Soul, the true self, accepts each new adventure, each new lifetime of learning. We are in physical bodies to learn certain lessons that help us move forward spiritually. Hopefully, the lessons we receive in each unique lifetime make us wiser, filling us with more love and compassion. These traits are needed to be of greater service to God, Soul's true mission and ultimate goal.

For more on this subject, read Linda C. Anderson's book, *35 Golden Keys to Who You Are & Why You're Here*.[2]

Soul is indestructible. The physical body may be hurt or killed, but Soul continues on, through lifetime after lifetime of experience. The play of karma (cause and effect) tempers and refines Soul. This

> You are Soul. You will never die, only your body will. Soul, the true self, accepts each new adventure, each new lifetime of learning.

tempering process prepares us for our destiny and makes us ready to serve God. To love as God loves. We then understand and have compassion for every side of every experience.

Karma is simply a way of learning a lesson. If you get the math problems wrong in school, you may fail the test. You learn from it and do better next time. We can view karma the same way.

Experiences with karma are often painful, but purifying. For example, in this life I lived alone and was lonely for many years due to a major past-life mistake. In that long-ago former life, as a petty tyrant, I had forced all in my kingdom to live alone until they found me a wife. In this life I had to experience the loneliness I caused for so many. Since I have been alone so much in this life, my heart is more open to the loneliness of others and I have found more compassion. It's an ongoing process, and understanding increases with each new lesson as I keep my heart open to God's love.

There is an old saying that "As ye sow, so shall ye reap." This is the same concept many people refer to as karma. It's simply a way of learning which deeds are beneficial to all life and which are destructive. Soul learns by watching the events It has caused and experiencing the effects. For example, a thief in a past life might be robbed in this life. The former thief now has the other side of the experience and learns how it feels.

Past-life recall helps us make sense of life. We get to see more clearly what situations have caused the karma we are currently experiencing.

There is an old saying that "As ye sow, so shall ye reap." This is the same concept many people refer to as karma.

Conversely, the difficult situations in our lives may give clues to past lives. For example: the person who continues to be robbed has a clue. She may examine the possibility she had taken what belonged to others in a past life. Such a discovery may not instantly erase the karma but may help her find a way to resolve it over time.

"Karma is removed naturally when the person is raised in spiritual awareness to the point where he realizes why he took it on in the first place," says Harold Klemp, author and expert on past lives. "Once you recognize what you did in spiritual ignorance to cause yourself a certain problem, in many cases the karmic burden can begin to work itself off."[3]

Harold Klemp is the spiritual leader of Eckankar and a modern-day prophet. I will refer to his work frequently. Of special interest is his book *Past Lives, Dreams, and Soul Travel*.[4] He offers eye-opening information on past lives and how we can access and use them to make spiritual headway today.

From his books and talks, I've learned many successful methods of working with past lives, as well as dreams and other spiritual techniques. As a spiritual being, he is my inner spiritual guide, called the Mahanta. He has the ability to comfort, protect, uplift, and give love in every situation. His mission is to lead Soul, by Its own path, home to God. Millions have benefited from his spiritual guidance. If you ask for his help inwardly, he will guide you through your past-life explorations.

Would you like to try a simple exercise right now to awaken to past lives in your dreams? The following

Harold Klemp is the spiritual leader of Eckankar and a modern-day prophet.

exercise is a gentle way to start your past-life exploration.

Exploration Exercise:

Dream-Time Discoveries

Tip: On Past-Life Study

To awaken past-life dreams, make a note of what things you greatly like or dislike. Do that also with people. Then watch your dreams. Also note if a certain country or century attracts you. There is a reason.

—Harold Klemp, *The Art of Spiritual Dreaming*[5]

If you would like to know more about working with dreams, study *The Art of Spiritual Dreaming* and my earlier book, *Dreams: Your Window to Heaven.*[6]

Sometimes a Soul has to live an entire lifetime with a certain karmic condition, such as a physical limitation or chronic illness.

Sometimes a Soul has to live an entire lifetime with a certain karmic condition, such as a physical limitation or chronic illness. The size and shape of our bodies may even be due to a karmic condition. I know of someone who has a very small body because, he says, in a former life he misused power. For another person the reason may be completely different. All karmic situations actually bring balance. Soul sets up these conditions before entering a new body in each new life, to teach It more about divine love. With love, Soul in any body can make Its way home to God.

Recognizing the root cause of any condition—whether physical, emotional, mental or spiritual—brings understanding, which in itself is a form of healing. Remembering past lives helps us understand the root cause of our spiritual lessons. Understanding our spiritual lessons brings us closer to God.

How do we know which past lives to explore?

Whatever is "up" for you in your life—whatever is really bothering, angering, or upsetting you in some way—is a good indicator of what to focus on for past-life exploration. It helps if you have someone you trust for inner guidance. You can ask God, the Holy Spirit, or the Mahanta to show you the past life you need to explore now to resolve or understand the issues that are presently plaguing you.

As I began working at recalling past lives, and discovering the root cause of challenges or habits in this life, I felt more free with each discovery. There was a definite feeling of lightness and love.

Exploring past lives has been a key for me to opening the door to the greatest love there is, God's love.

In addition to continuing to heal old wounds and solve present problems, I now view studying my past lives as a means to removing roadblocks in the way of receiving and giving divine, unconditional love.

Exploring past lives has been a key for me to opening the door to the greatest love there is, God's love.

PAST-LIFE RECALLS CAN HELP US SEE LOVE IN THE MOST DIFFICULT SITUATIONS

Forgiveness is a big key to seeing love where there appears to be none. I at times found it very difficult to forgive some people in my life for past hurts. But when I forgave them, miracles happened.

I finally felt able to give those individuals love and got more love in return.

Others have had this same experience. Laura tells her past-life story, which she discovered through a spiritual exercise, sometimes called contemplation.

I had a fear of a certain editor I worked with. Maybe you can imagine someone being afraid of an editor's corrections. That's understandable. But this level of fear was ridiculous. I was afraid of something more. I couldn't even accept invitations to spend time with her, feeling that somehow I would be criticized for my every thought, word, and deed! What was my problem?

Finally one day, after much contemplation on this topic and working with spiritual exercises, I realized a connection from the past. She had been in a position of power in a past life and had taken my life, not just edited my writing! I had written something then that offended the authority of the time, and it was her job to carry out "justice".

My spiritual lesson was to see that I, too, have been in positions of power and authority in past lives. Whether fair or not, I have also delivered what was then called justice, in my own way.

I inwardly forgave my editor for the role she played in our previous life. I forgave myself for the similar roles I've played, and the love in my heart returned. Now I could feel love for her because the fear was gone. She has become a dear friend, and I gain so much from her wisdom.

> My spiritual lesson was to see that I, too, have been in positions of power and authority in past lives.

Relationships Can Be Healed through Remembering Past Lives

Life is a series of relationships that help us grow spiritually and often work out karma at the same time—whether we are aware of it or not. Understanding the spiritual lessons in a relationship, as Laura did, is easier through past-life recall. The insights we gain also bring about a healing, sometimes quickly, sometimes slowly.

Like many married couples, my former husband and I ran into difficult patterns.

*O*ne day I realized we must have had many lives together. By listening to God during my daily spiritual exercise, I discovered one lifetime in particular was creating problems in this life. I felt as though I couldn't say no to helping him, even though I was already very busy.

In one of our past lives together, I was among his indentured servants. My family owed him money and had no way of repaying it. I was homely in that life and likely had no chance of marriage. So my parents offered me, their eldest daughter, to work off the debt.

As soon as I remembered that life, I asked my husband if I could share it with him. He agreed and confirmed that he had definitely been in such a position. It carried over into this life, and he found it quite natural to delegate certain tasks to me.

Before I was aware of our past life together, I offered to help my husband quite often, when I should

Life is a series of relationships that help us grow spiritually and often work out karma at the same time—whether we are aware of it or not.

have been focusing on my own responsibilities. Once I realized what I was doing and why, it actually helped us both work more toward our own individual missions in life. In addition, I was able to clear out my guilt for not being able to work for him full time. You can imagine how much this improved our connection with each other! Feeling more love and respect for each other brought us closer to God.

Health Issues May Be Resolved—or At Least Better Understood—When Old Lifetimes Are Uncovered

Loving ourselves is important too, especially when it comes to health. Respecting our bodies as temples for God, we want to maintain health as best we can. Sometimes the method for healing old physical problems eludes us, until we discover that the cause goes further back than this present life.

Pain often drives us to dig deeper to find the spiritual lesson, for real spiritual healing. Healing of the physical body can be a side benefit of exploring past lives.

Seventeen-year-old Anna helped resolve a health issue by exploring her past. She says:

> Pain often drives us to dig deeper to find the spiritual lesson, for real spiritual healing.

At my young age, I have knee problems, even though I'm not athletic. In a past life I got hit by an arrow in my knee. I remember this each time I get shooting pains through this area.

The image I see in my mind is of me riding a horse. I was Cherokee and at war with one of our rival tribes when I was hit by the arrow. I felt so badly then, because I would no longer be of use to my tribe, to help protect my family. I pushed myself hard in that life, and I still do in this one.

Unexplained aches and pains like Anna's may be past-life injuries or karmic debts being repaid. Since first speaking with Anna, there's been a happy ending. At first, Anna could no longer run or dance as she used to. But because of an acceptance of her physical limitations, she was becoming more relaxed with life, not pushing herself so hard, as she had in her Cherokee lifetime.

Anna finally had a doctor examine her knee, and he prescribed surgery. Confirmation about her past-life injury came when the surgeon later handed her a small piece of bone that had separated from her knee and caused the problem. It was shaped like an arrowhead! Able to run and dance again, Anna is thrilled with her progress.

How can we heal problems created by ancient karma?

Through love, the most powerful spiritual tool we have. If we can love and forgive ourselves—and forgive anyone we believe has wronged us—we can heal the pain or illness more easily. Even if we have to live with the pain or illness awhile longer, this forgiveness brings us closer to God, closer to love.

> How can we heal problems created by ancient karma? Through love, the most powerful spiritual tool we have.

FEARS AND PHOBIAS MAY DISAPPEAR WITH PAST-LIFE RECALL

Getting closer to God's love is so much easier when we can let go of fear. Though not always an easy project, the effort is often well rewarded, as it was for me in the story to follow. Unfounded fears and unexplained phobias can cause health problems as well, filtering from the emotional to the physical level. A past-life memory may provide the understanding to begin the healing.

I have had intense anxiety most of my life. Unable to ever completely relax, I felt most anxious in the kitchen. This feeling of fear and panic heightened whenever I cooked for guests.

Why?

I knew the strong emotions I was feeling definitely did not come from this lifetime. My mother was an accomplished cook and entertained quite often, in a very relaxed manner. I never felt tension from her in those situations or from any other relatives or friends who entertained. When I entertained, however, I was always in a panic.

Where did I learn to be this tense in the kitchen? What caused the panic?

One day I decided to do a spiritual exercise to discover the cause of this fear. I've learned in Eckankar that spiritual exercises are the doorway to the spiritual worlds. They can help us see ourselves as the beautiful, bright, eternal beings we are. *The Spiritual Exercises of ECK*,[7] by Harold Klemp, has over a hundred spiritual exercises you can try.

Spiritual exercises open us to our potential as Soul and move us forward spiritually. They may also show us our own future or past, if we ask with an open, loving heart. The *exploration exercises* given in

I've learned in Eckankar that spiritual exercises are the doorway to the spiritual worlds. They can help us see ourselves as the beautiful, bright, eternal beings we are.

this book are spiritual exercises, which can be creative and changed to fit your own needs. A simple spiritual exercise is to sing the ancient love song to God, HU. It is pronounced like the word *hue* and sung in a long, drawn-out breath (HU-u-u-u). If done for fifteen to twenty minutes each day, it will bring you closer to God and fill your life with more love.

HU is also God's love song to us. We can hear it in every sound. This is the sound of God calling us home. When we sing this love song to God, it is like saying "I love you, God" and "Thy will be done."

When I did this spiritual exercise, I simply asked the Mahanta, my inner guide to show me what lifetime may have caused me to feel this unfounded fear and panic when I prepared a meal for guests.

Hu is also God's love song to us. We can hear it in every sound. This is the sound of God calling us home.

I found myself watching a scene and being a part of it at the same time. I was standing in an ancient kitchen, cooking for a royal feast. The king was entertaining foreign royalty. I was the head chef and responsible for every detail of the meal. The fear was overwhelming in that life; I could be beheaded for failing to create the meal his majesty had expected to impress his important guests.

The king was angry about the fact that his royal guests had not agreed with an idea he had proposed. I was handy and made a good scapegoat. There was nothing he could do about his guests' reactions, but he could do anything he wanted with me. I was therefore blamed for the failed dinner party, and my life was shortened immediately!

Having been a cruel monarch myself in other lifetimes, my demise was well deserved. But the panic of having my head cut off for cooking carried into lifetime after lifetime until I had the awareness to ask for help and accept it.

Over time, my feelings of anxiety in the kitchen lessened. Now I am much more relaxed when preparing meals for company!

OVERCOMING FEAR OF DEATH

Death is one of the most common fears.

The answer to the question What's the worst thing that can happen? is usually death. But if you know there is really no such thing as death, you can take the risk of exploring this life fully and enjoying it now.

> Healing the fear of death has helped me live life more fully, because there is nothing more to fear.

Healing the fear of death has helped me live life more fully, because there is nothing more to fear. I now can do things I may not have attempted before.

As Soul we can never die, so we keep reuniting with loved ones from our past. Glen's pleasant past-life recall shows how Soul and love live on eternally.

I began a relationship with Lisa when I was in college. I didn't know why I was with Lisa, because I was Jewish and she was of another faith. I had a dream one night that revealed our connection from a past life.

The image in the dream was a man and wife standing on a mountain pass in China. She was an old woman and I was an old man, but I had to leave China immediately. I had said or done something wrong and would have been killed had I stayed.

It was heartbreaking for us to have to separate, but I could not allow her to face the dangers of the mountains in winter. I told her I wouldn't see her again in that life but promised to find her in the next. Because of my advanced age, I died of exposure and hunger in the mountains.

In the dream I was speaking a Chinese language, but somehow I knew the words in English when I awoke from the dream.

Now I knew why I wanted to be with Lisa. I had made a promise and had to fulfill it.

Glen told me he learned from this inner experience that Souls who have made a promise to each other can always find each other no matter where in the universe they might be. That past-life memory awakened him to the fleeting experience of death as simply a rite of passage for Soul. Now he knows Soul never dies. It just continues to transform from lifetime to lifetime until It finally returns to God as a mature spiritual being.

Sometimes, happily, old karma is good karma. When we've done a kindness without interfering, it may help someone else move forward spiritually. This comes back to us in a pleasant way as good karma. Soul learns from this too.

Unfortunately, many of us are not as willing to change until a tough lesson comes along. Pain and trauma from difficult lessons may accompany death. Difficult emotions might carry over to the next life with each death. They may build fear in us that we have to remove. Why? Because fear, especially the sort that comes up again and again, separates us from God.

When we've done a kindness without interfering, it may help someone else move forward spiritually. This comes back to us in a pleasant way as good karma.

LETTING GO OF FEAR
BRINGS US CLOSER TO GOD

Finding out about past lives, for me, has been like finding a golden key to an old suitcase full of unconscious fear that has weighed me down for centuries. I feel so much lighter every time I pull out a past-life memory that has been hiding inside me, waiting to scare me into unconsciously acting or reacting a certain way. When I remove and heal the old image, I remember more of who I really am. Then I can remember what I am here for—to learn to love. To become love.

We already *are* love, we already *are* part of God, but it's so easy to forget. Removing the fear can help us remember this truth.

Each lifetime challenges us to open our hearts to more and more love. When we've mastered that, we are released from the wheel of rebirths and can finally return to the heavenly worlds as Co-workers with God, or continue to serve God in a fuller capacity here on earth.

What's a Co-worker with God?

"Once we have learned to let the ECK [Holy Spirit] work through us all the time, we then become a Co-worker with God," says Harold Klemp. "The person who is learning to become a co-worker with life gives divine love back to life. He has learned to be grateful for the blessings that come to him."[8]

A mature, experienced Soul is a pure vehicle for God's love, and God will work with that vehicle to help other Souls unfold and mature. The mission of

> Each lifetime challenges us to open our hearts to more and more love.

Soul is to become this loving Co-worker with God.

How can we remember who we really are as Soul, a divine particle of God?

Singing HU, the ancient love song to God explained earlier in this chapter, can help us experience this higher state of awareness.

Another way to become more aware as Soul is to explore the many faces we've worn, to see that they were just roles, not who we really are. But believing we are these roles can get in the way of the precious memory of being Soul. These illusionary experiences, however necessary for our spiritual unfoldment, have kept us from remembering our true missions, to become loving Co-workers with God.

To remember we are love may mean removing the many masks that we've become attached to. Exploring past lives can help us let go of them.

If your relationships, career, finances, health, or other experiences in your life feel unbalanced in any way or if you experience an emotional reaction that doesn't make sense to you, you may be subconsciously responding to a past life.

To remember we are love may mean removing the many masks that we've become attached to. Exploring past lives can help us let go of them.

HOW CAN WE BEST EXPLORE PAST LIVES?

There are several effective methods for past-life exploration, the simplest of which is working with your dreams, as in the exercise given earlier in this chapter. There is also intuition. You might sense truth in a movie, novel, historical writing, or documentary.

The most important thing is to trust yourself to hear or see the answers correctly. Trusting the connection you have with God, with Holy Spirit, with whatever you believe is guiding your spiritual affairs, is paramount to success in this endeavor.

When you try one of the exercises in this book to explore a past life, you may want to begin by choosing a situation that has been bothering you in this life, especially if it has been a pattern or an ongoing concern, e.g., a fear of heights or a dislike of certain people or places. Begin with a simple problem to gently open yourself to the truth of your past and how it may be affecting you now.

Try the exploration exercise below to practice opening yourself to the possibility of a past-life recall via intuition. If there is any fear about remembering your past lives, you may find that working with this exercise helps to eliminate fear, especially if you don't expect results right away but allow them to come naturally over the course of the next few days or weeks, in a dream or in daily life.

Imagination is the key to past-life exercises. Whatever you imagine, whatever comes to you, is real to you in some way. It exists somewhere inside you, or you wouldn't be able to imagine it! If you say to yourself, "This is just my imagination!" you can say right back to yourself, "That's right, and it's real."

> Imagination is the key to past-life exercises. Whatever you imagine, whatever comes to you, is real to you in some way.

Exploration Exercise: Karma as a Clue

1. Write down any situation which occurs over and over again in your life. For example: "I've never kept a job for more than a year," or "I can

never seem to find the money to buy new clothes."

2. Now rephrase the pattern in the third person, to get a higher, or Soul, perspective, as if you were an observer. For example: "He's never kept a job for more than a year" or "She's never able to find the money to buy new clothes."

3. Ask for help from God or whomever you look to spiritually. You may want to try singing HU, as described previously, to uplift yourself and see from the higher viewpoint of Soul. Seeing from a higher spiritual view is like seeing from a bird's-eye view. Instead of being in the middle of the problem, you rise above it to see all the pieces of the puzzle and how they fit together to give you your answer, to show you the spiritual lesson or give you a new direction.

From this lofty view, look to see what possible past-life situation may have created the undesirable pattern in this present life. Write down anything that comes to mind. Even if it seems like you are imagining it or making it up, write it anyway! It will likely still have much value in unraveling your previous patterns. It always has for me.

If nothing comes to you, let it be. Watch your dreams and your daily life for more clues. It may come to you over time or in a flash. Be open to the answer coming to you in any way God chooses to bring it.

Instead of being in the middle of the problem, you rise above it to see all the pieces of the puzzle and how they fit together to give you your answer, to show you the spiritual lesson or give you a new direction.

WHAT HAPPENS WHEN YOU REMEMBER A PAST LIFE?

Past-life recall can tune you in to the reasons for your concerns, fears, and patterns as shown in the stories in this chapter. It can help you heal those old patterns as well, when you are able to let go.

There have been times when I was unable to let go of a past life. I felt righteous indignation for having been victimized by certain kinds of people. For example, in a lifetime where I was a slave, raped and beaten by my owner (who also took my children away to sell to other slave owners and killed my husband too), I vowed I would never let a white man touch me again. In this life I was born white, yet was always much more attracted to dark-skinned friends. When I recalled that past life, I completely understood this inclination!

But I had not forgiven my perpetrators nor healed my wounds from that lifetime. I had not let go. Later on I realized I had also been a slave master, in charge of the Jewish slaves for the pharaoh in Egypt. I revisited my African-American slave life with this new knowledge of myself as a previous slave owner.

Once I saw these past lives from the higher viewpoint of Soul, I was finally able to fully forgive my slave owner and let go.

The next chapter will give you several methods to explore the past lives that may be holding you back in this one.

> Past-life recall can tune you in to the reasons for your concerns, fears, and patterns.

2

Uncovering the Mysterious Past

*There are few individuals who really want
to know who and what they are; the majority of
people are afraid to face and master their short-
comings. But that's the key to spiritual strength.*

— Harold Klemp,
Autobiography of a Modern Prophet[1]

———————

$\mathcal{W}$hy don't we just remember all of our past lives automatically each time we're born?

We are shielded from remembering them because we'd be overwhelmed by so many images, thoughts, and experiences. If we remembered every life we've had, the mental and emotional trauma and strain would prevent us from doing what we are here to do now—live *this* life and fully partake of its experience. Remembering one or two past lives at a time is quite enough for most people, when they are ready to expand their awareness this way.

But many of us have unconsciously blocked memories of any other lifetime, and we just as unconsciously live as the effect of these unexplored

If we remembered every life we've had, the mental and emotional trauma and strain would prevent us from doing what we are here to do now—live *this* life and fully partake of its experience.

experiences. So the goal of this book is to answer the question: How can we most easily explore past lives?

In the previous chapter we covered several methods for discovering past lives, such as dreams, spiritual exercises, and intuition—simply paying attention to life. But the best results come by asking for help from Holy Spirit, God, the Mahanta, or who you look to as your inner spiritual teacher.

Spiritual guidance keeps us balanced and safe as we explore the jungle of past experiences. It's like going on a safari in a remote part of Africa; you would probably like to have a guide along to protect you from harm and lead you to the sights you came to see.

The same protection and spiritual insights come when you work with a spiritual guide experienced in this area.

My inner guide, the Mahanta, has helped me find so much insight into my past lives. Having the Mahanta as my spiritual guide has helped me to become more aware of my own spirituality. This divine connection gives me love, protection, and guidance every single day of my life. Working with such a qualified inner guide can do the same for you.

You may have already met the Mahanta. He is the embodiment of God's love, appearing to some as a blue star or blue light. He is here to assist all Souls who ask for his help. Feel free to call upon him, as Moira did in the next story you'll read.

My inner guide, the Mahanta, has helped me find so much insight into my past lives.

WHEN FEAR IS SET ASIDE,
LOVE CAN FILL ITS PLACE

Moira used an exercise for past-life recall to accept the marriage she had always yearned for.

Moira was dating Gordon, a wonderful man, and knew the next step was marriage. But she didn't feel ready. Funny, because this was what she had always wanted, someone like Gordon who promised to support and take care of her. But for some strange, unknown reason, she feared this commitment.

She needed to find out what was in the way of her moving forward. After doing a spiritual exercise in which she asked for help from the Mahanta regarding her unfounded fear, one of Moira's past lives emerged:

Moira used an exercise for past-life recall to accept the marriage she had always yearned for.

As I was working in the fields, I was swept up onto a horse and kidnapped. Then I was taken to a stone tower and locked in. I was to serve my master as a concubine. Even though I was given all I needed, I was never free again. As a peasant, I'd had no expectation of a great marriage, but I had freedom. My capture was heartbreaking. I was never to see my family again and had to do my master's bidding.

Moira says that once she became aware of that past life, she was freed of her fear, knowing that was then and this is now. She was now a completely different person in completely different circumstances. Moira's unconscious, fearful image of that past life was resolved simply by her conscious memory of it. She dismissed the image as a dead and useless memory, keeping only the compassion learned. In just a few days, Moira received a marriage proposal from Gordon. She accepted gladly and gratefully, with no fear attached!

Throughout this book, you'll find examples of past-life discovery techniques. Some will focus on asking the Mahanta for help. You will see how simple it can be.

SHARING YOUR EXPERIENCES WITH OTHERS

To help make your experience the best it can be, here are three suggestions to keep in mind when researching past lives.

The first suggestion is to be very careful about sharing your experience with others. They may not be ready to accept your insights and may judge you without thinking. This is particularly important when you have discovered a past life involving someone you know. If you were to tell the other person without their permission, they may not be ready to hear it, and it may upset them.

I took the experience as a lesson to be careful about what I said to others regarding *my* past lives.

This happened to me. Someone told me about a lifetime in a nunnery where she remembered me being an older nun who was quite cruel to her. This was *her* experience. I don't recall that lifetime. I was very new to recalling past lives at the time, and it upset me. Her insight was for her, not me. I thought of this woman as a friend and respected her, so I never told her how I felt since it didn't come up again. However, I took the experience as a lesson to be careful about what I said to others regarding *my* past lives.

Which Lifetimes Should I Explore?

The second suggestion is to ask yourself this question. Which lifetimes do I want to explore and why?

We may like to explore past lives to find when we were the hero. But if the goal is to learn truth and grow spiritually, we do better focusing on lifetimes that may be in the way of our spiritual unfoldment, or ones holding us back in any aspect of our lives. These are not easy to look at, especially if we were the rogues or villains in that life.

A wise friend said we all want to be heroes in our past lives. She's right. It took me a long time to face the fact that I had been morally corrupt and full of my own importance in many lives. At times I selfishly wielded power. These were the lifetimes that *caused* the victim lifetimes I remember with much more ease. Yes, I wanted to be a hero, or at least a victim, but I healed much faster from discovering and accepting lifetimes as a villain.

The good news is, you're not alone. None of us have been perfect angels. If you wish to heal yourself and unfold spiritually, look for the full range of lifetimes. They contain the seeds of your entire experience, from start to finish, from a cause in a past life to the effect in this life.

> If you wish to heal yourself and unfold spiritually, look for the full range of lifetimes. They contain the seeds of your entire experience, from start to finish, from a cause in a past life to the effect in this life.

Thy Will Be Done

The third suggestion is to ask for help from God or the Holy Spirit. We can receive guidance from the highest viewpoint of life—the best and broadest view, like the eagle's view, higher than we could possibly see ourselves. When we're not sure where to look or what to look for, we can always get a spiritual boost by opening ourselves to the Holy Spirit.

I ask the Mahanta for help and say, "Thy will be done." Saying "Thy will be done" helps me let go and surrender the outcome to God. This opens me to the insights I need from the highest spiritual viewpoint, helping me forgive myself and others as needed.

Asking for help from God can bring whatever is the next step in achieving spiritual balance.

One person was seeing too many of his own past lives, and even other people's past lives. It got so bad that he had difficulty focusing on his own present-time life. He found the teachings of Eckankar and asked the Mahanta for help. Soon he was relieved of this unbalanced situation.

Everyone gets help when they ask, but the amount of help will be according to their karmic situation and lessons needed. Another person may have more to learn from that particular situation, so they will get help in understanding it better or handling it better spiritually. Each situation is individual, according to karma. (You may be surprised at how much help you get when you ask!)

You don't have to be a member of Eckankar to ask the Mahanta for help, but you must ask him for help if you want it. The Mahanta will not interfere with your freedom of choice.

Everyone gets help when they ask, but the amount of help will be according to their karmic situation and lessons needed.

TRUST YOURSELF AND YOUR CONNECTION WITH THE HOLY SPIRIT

Trust yourself that you will recognize the answers you need. You may have forgotten them, or they may be buried deep within you. When you are remembering details or images of a past life, it may feel like it's just your imagination. But, whatever you imagine exists. If a particular answer is valid for you, it will ring true when you hear it. Pieces of your life's puzzle may also fall into place then, giving you more validation for your memories.

> Trust yourself that you will recognize the answers you need. If a particular answer is valid for you, it will ring true when you hear it.

WATCHING PAST-LIFE IMAGES

The simplest method for recalling a past life is watching the images that come to you and trusting them.

When I asked why my mother was so critical and I was so defensive, an image of the Spanish Inquisition arose. I started by trusting the image. It could be real. If I assumed it was real, then I only had to ask myself, Was I the inquisitor or the prisoner? I was likely the inquisitor, as much as I dislike thinking of it!

The images that come to you may be valid, so trust them initially until you know for sure whether or not they are. This gives you a chance to get used to them while exploring further, rather than avoiding a hard lesson.

As Soul, you keep pictures stored away to look at any time you wish, any time you are ready. Would you like to look at some now? Here's a specific exercise to do so.

Exploration Exercise:
Past-Life Recall with Images

1. To begin from a higher viewpoint, ask for guidance from God or the Mahanta. Think of a specific situation that bothers you. Allow yourself to feel that sense of being bothered by it. Perhaps it's an unexplained fear, an attraction, or misplaced anger. Any emotion you feel around this situation can be the link to your past. Let yourself feel this feeling now.

2. Open your mind to the possibility of a past life attached to this feeling. Allow any images to come to mind.

3. Note what images come to you—write them down or draw them. You may not necessarily get images, but a sense, an intuitive feeling or knowing. Just for now, jot down or draw anything that comes to you, no matter how crazy or out-of-this-world it seems.

4. Look at your notes, and look at your life. Does anything you wrote make sense in relation to the emotions or actions around this issue in your present life? If so, note that as well.

   If your answers or images don't make sense yet, let them rest. Try this technique again, or try some of the others in this chapter. Past-life recall often comes in bits and pieces. Allow the process to happen in its own time, as you are ready to accept it.

Past-life recall often comes in bits and pieces. Allow the process to happen in its own time, as you are ready to accept it.

The previous exercise works well for me when I really trust myself and go with the first image that comes to mind. Here's one confirmation that tickled me when I got it.

I was dating a man in a different city whom I'll call Fred. I had been attracted to Fred immediately through a video of him I'd seen at a dating service. After just one visit with him, conflict arose. I didn't understand why he spoke to me in such a commanding way or why I resented it so much.

To understand this conflict better, I did the exercise just given, allowing images to come to mind. I saw a Viking ship with Viking warriors on board. I explored further by looking at the images I already had, asking for guidance from the Mahanta, and allowing more images to come to mind. I saw that Fred was my superior and I was a lower-ranking leader. The other Vikings on the ship looked to me, however, for friendship. I was good at listening in that life, and Fred was not. His jealousy finally overcame him, and he threw me overboard, ending my life.

After this vision, my first thought was, *That's ridiculous!* In fact, that's the first thing I always seem to think when I see a new past-life image! I asked God for confirmation, and here's what happened:

The very next morning a friend insisted we go to breakfast out in the country. We stopped at a restaurant neither of us had ever seen before. It was called The Nordic Crossing. I knew this was part of my answer, but it still felt silly. Yet I knew it was time to face facts when I

After this vision, my first thought was, *That's ridiculous!* In fact, that's the first thing I always seem to think when I see a new past-life image! I asked God for confirmation.

walked into the restaurant. Facing me squarely as I turned was a full-size wooden statue of a very fierce-looking Viking!

EVEN IF IT FEELS RIDICULOUS, IT MAY BE TRUE

How do you know if what you see or remember is really one of your past lives?

One past-life-therapy researcher, Morris Netherton, has a theory about remembering past lives. He tells us that when you have a strong emotion associated with the image of a past life, there is a likelihood it's real.[3] Another expert, Hans Tendam, says you don't necessarily have to experience the emotional aspect of a past life.[4]

I have certainly experienced past-life recall without feeling the emotion, and later I had validation from the Holy Spirit, as I just shared in my Viking story. You can assure yourself of the authenticity of your past-life memory by simply asking God to show you verification of your experience through your daily life or dreams. Once you have the secure feeling that you know, you can test it by looking at your present life. Ask:

- Does this new knowledge help you in some way?
- Does it heal any situations or give you more insight?

Another way of validating a past-life experience is to study the details of the culture, laws, dress, customs, and history of the time you remember. This was done in the case of Bridey Murphy. She was the famous Colorado homemaker regressed through

> You can assure yourself of the authenticity of your past-life memory by simply asking God to show you verification of your experience through your daily life or dreams.

hypnosis into a past life as an Irish woman. Research was done to determine if details of her life, culture, and time were correct. These details were sometimes individual to her small village. Many were verified and found to be true.[5]

You may find other ways of assuring yourself that your past-life recall is real. The bottom line is this: if it freed you from fear in this life, whatever you remembered has complete validity in your world. How you experience your past-life memory is truly individual.

You may not always see things as images. Not everyone is visual. Some people hear things, and some may feel or sense an experience from a past life. This is what happened to Eileen:

> *E*very time it rained, my sister Denise thought it would flood and we would all die. I never felt like she did about thunderstorms until one summer when I was older.
>
> After going to see a play about a flood, there was a huge thunderstorm. I stood at the window watching the lightning and listening to the thunder with dread in my heart. Never before had I felt this way—very frightened, not knowing what would happen.
>
> Part of me was observing this unusual fear thinking, *This is ridiculous!* Then I got hold of myself and thought, *This must be connected to a past life. Rain has never caused problems for me in this life.* As soon as I had the thought, I knew my sister Denise and I had been together in a terrible flood in a past life. We were warned to leave, but we didn't listen or didn't have time

If it freed you from fear in this life, whatever you remembered has complete validity in your world. How you experience your past-life memory is truly individual.

to get out. Our home was gone, and most of our loved ones with it. We were devastated.

As I relived this memory, I felt it would all be OK now, as if I was healed.

My sister had carried the fear of thunderstorms consciously but didn't know why she had it. Even though I had suppressed my fear over many lives, it surfaced when I was ready to handle it. The play about the flood was the trigger.

When I had this experience, I could feel all the feelings being passed off. I was able to let go of something holding me back, likely the guilt or fear about not listening when we were warned to clear out.

> I was able to let go of something holding me back, likely the guilt or fear about not listening when we were warned.

Eileen was able to let herself experience a past life from a feeling. The feeling of the flood was predominant. The images were secondary and came later as she allowed the experience to surface. You can do this too.

ARE YOU READY?

Perhaps you've been reading along, enjoying the stories and exercises but hesitant to jump in. What if you don't see anything? What if it doesn't work for you?

I was hesitant the first time I tried to remember a past life, but more surprising is I *still* feel hesitant at times, even after twenty-five years of working with past lives! Each situation is different. Perhaps I don't want to relive a certain experience due to its pain or discomfort. Perhaps I don't want to know how dreadful I was as a personality in the past.

When I get to the point where the pain in this present life is unbearable, it pushes me to go back to my past. So being ready hasn't been my strong point. I give myself time to do this as I feel inclined. You may want to be kind to yourself and give yourself the time you need as well.

This next exercise allows you to explore a possible past life without expecting images to surface. If they do, great! If they don't, there is still a great chance you will get some benefit.

Exploration Exercise: Sensing Past Lives

1. Ask yourself what fear might be holding you back. Feel this fear now as you think about, listen to, or sense the situation that causes it in this life.

2. Allow the feeling of this fear to expand into the past, as if you are reaching back in time with your emotion.

3. Ask God to allow you to sense or feel the life you may have lived that caused this fear. You may feel something, hear something, or have an intuitive feeling about this former life.

4. Trust yourself to know the answer that is right for you. The more you trust yourself and your imagination or intuition, the more sure you'll be when you remember one of your past lives. You may know by the feeling that comes over you—a feeling of just knowing or perhaps a sense of being lighter and more free.

The more you trust yourself and your imagination or intuition, the more sure you'll be when you remember one of your past lives.

DREAMS CAN TAKE YOU PLACES YOU'VE NEVER BEEN BEFORE

Another way to explore past lives is through dreams. This is a great method for those who like to keep a dream journal. Logging my dreams has helped me immeasurably. I am so grateful for the answers I have received in dreams, from the next career move to relationship issues.

Keeping a dream journal is a simple way to begin remembering your dreams. Keep the journal right next to your bed, within easy reach, if you should awaken during the night. A small flashlight taped to a pen is handy so as not to disturb a mate or wake yourself up too much. You may find you're already remembering past lives in dreams, but you were not looking at them that way.

Dreams are a doorway to many levels of heaven— present, past, and future.

> Dreams are a doorway to many levels of heaven— present, past, and future.

Exploration Exercise:

Looking for Past Lives in Dreams

1. Just before sleep, write a question in your dream journal or notebook. This could be related to any unusual situation you suspect may come from a past life.

2. Write down anything you remember as soon as you wake up. You may only remember one word, image, or feeling. For example, *man* or *tiger.* You may write, "I feel sad." Anything you write is a clue. Mark these pages to look at

later. Writing anything you can will help the flow of dream memory improve each day.

3. Look at the dreams, or pieces of dreams, from the eye of eternal Soul. This means to open yourself to the possibility that one or more of your dreams may be a past life you experienced. Remember, once you open yourself to this possibility, you will know if it is a past-life recall.

4. Try this exercise every night until you have results. Give yourself a few weeks, then take a break to let go a bit. A good attitude is, Thy will be done. This allows God to work with you, unhindered by human expectations.

> Writing anything you can will help the flow of dream memory improve each day.

Here is an example of someone who used dreams to explore past lives. Steven journeyed into his past in a series of three dreams showing him why he felt so protective of one of his high-school classmates.

In the first dream I was a descendent of a slave and a Confederate Army officer in the United States Civil War. It was a painful time for me. There was a break in the war. I found out my dog and some of my best friends had gotten shot and killed.

This faded into the next dream.

I was a wealthy African-American in the 1930s in Peoria, Illinois. I was happily married and loved my family. Belonging to a local business circle, I felt good about myself. I was an honest entrepreneur, but I knew my life was in danger because I was black. With this knowledge,

I put all my affairs in order, though I didn't tell my wife. I did get killed in that life just for being successful and being black.

One more dream followed.

I was a nine-year-old boy running through a warehouse. I knew the white men chasing me hated me because I was black. They were going to kill me. I was hiding under boxes of lumber, when everything went dark. I had been shot and killed.

In each life there was something I loved, and it was hard to let go of life.

After these dreams, I understood my openness and acceptance of each and every Soul. The dreams helped me see I had lived other lifetimes in a variety of races. I also knew why I never wanted to mistreat another human being like I had been mistreated.

It then made sense that I had always defended the one African-American boy in my high-school class of six hundred. He always got picked on, and my heart went out to him. I felt he was unjustly treated. Even though we never became friends or even spent any time together, I still felt strongly about stepping in to help him.

> He was more courageous because of his previous incarnations, even before consciously remembering them. His greater acceptance of others now expands his circle of love.

Steven's unpleasant dreams of former lives explained why he had always opened his heart to others in this life. He was more courageous because of his previous incarnations, even before consciously remembering them. His greater acceptance of others now expands his circle of love.

If you want to expand your own circle of love and explore more of life than you can imagine exists, you may want to study your dreams. Dreams are real. They are experiences Soul is having while your body is sleeping. They may not always come through clearly, like Steven's did, but you can piece them together with practice.

Past-life dreams may come unbidden, so when you have a dream that seems like a movie of someone else's life, and it has strong emotions for you, write it down. Continue to ask the Holy Spirit for guidance as you look for answers to past lives in your dreams or elsewhere.

When you're unsure about answers you get regarding past lives, you can always ask God!

THE CHOICES WE MAKE CAN BRING FREEDOM

Anna tried asking for God's help in a spiritual exercise with great results.

Anna began to experience a sharp pain in her upper back, just about the time she was meeting her family for a reunion. She didn't have time to visit her doctor before she left. Being very aware of past-life possibilities, she decided to try the following spiritual exercise to explore the cause of this pain. It is a simple exercise you can use as well:

Exploration Exercise:

Ask God to Show You

1. Ask God to show you the past life, if there is one, that relates to your health problem or any other issue in your life right now. If you wish, you may ask the Mahanta, as explained in chapter 1.

Past-life dreams may come unbidden, so when you have a dream that seems like a movie of someone else's life, and it has strong emotions for you, write it down.

He will help you if you ask. The Mahanta can see all of your past lives and may show you the one you need to see, if you are ready.

2. Close your eyes, looking and listening for an answer.

3. Accept the answer you get as possible truth for just one day. See what happens after that. You may get some verification or simply see the pieces fall into place as you remember incidents, talents, or skills from your present life.

When Anna asked God for an answer and listened, here's what she heard and how she handled it:

Where my back hurt was a feeling of being stabbed in the back. As I did a spiritual exercise, I got the impression I was once born into a powerful family. We were definitely in the public eye. Being youngest and more popular with the people, I was a threat to my other family members. One of them finally stabbed me in the back with a knife and killed me. Everyone in that family is now a member of my family in this life.

After this realization, I was preparing to meet my family for dinner. We were staying in different hotels, so we had to arrange where to meet. Somehow I missed the messages they left for me, so I didn't know what time or where we were to meet.

I sat in the lobby for two hours, feeling angry and sad about my family having turned against

Where my back hurt was a feeling of being stabbed in the back. As I did a spiritual exercise, I got the impression I was once born into a powerful family.

me in a past life. I said to myself, *No, I'm not going to dinner.*

I thought about this more and decided I could hold on to my resentment, to being right, or choose to forgive. I realized it was my choice in the present to release it to love. Ultimately love won, and I contacted a member of my family, learned where they were meeting, and went to dinner.

Now my family and I get along much better, and I try to stay aware of my feelings from the past.

TRUSTING WHAT YOU KNOW

One more simple technique for remembering past lives is just knowing. Knowing your intuition works!

It took me awhile to trust that I really knew the answers to my past-life questions. Now I simply trust the feelings or hazy images, acting as if they are true until I can get a clear answer. It always amazes me how well these feelings fit.

It takes practice to trust yourself more, but it's worth it. You can use your intuition to move forward spiritually through discovering past lives. Here's a technique to just know:

One more simple technique for remembering past lives is just knowing. Knowing your intuition works!

Exploration Exercise:

Trusting What You Know

1. Choose a situation you would like to resolve. This should be an issue you've already tried to clear up using conventional means. You may

> already suspect the cause of the problem comes from a past life.

2. Ask yourself what you already know. Do you have any kind of sense about what a past-life connection might be? If not, make something up! I know this sounds outrageous, but it works almost every time.

   Act as if you are telling someone a story about a past life you lived.

3. Write it down or record it on audiocassette to make sure you capture all the images or feelings.

You may be amazed at how closely the story fits the situation then and now. You will also find validation in your present life.

Jessica was finding it difficult to speak up for herself. She resolved this through trusting her intuition about a past life she had:

Whenever someone said, "Speak up!" I wanted to hide. I usually just shut up. I wanted to get past this awful feeling. It seemed to me I was unimportant or what I had to say was nothing anyone would want to hear. These feelings couldn't have come from this lifetime. Everyone in my family was outspoken. Not one of them was shy, and they encouraged me to talk or sing as well.

I wanted to explore the past-life possibilities for my hesitancy to speak.

All I could come up with was, "I don't know, I just don't know."

Then I tried this exercise, and it worked! I told myself a story, as if I was telling a child, and came up with the real thing. Here's the story I told myself:

I was being choked, unable to speak. I wanted desperately to speak, so that I could clear my name of wrongdoing. I died before I could explain that I didn't kill his brother! Someone else killed him and blamed it on me, because I was just a lowly servant. I was very slow mentally and could not get my words out in time to save myself.

It amazed me how accurate this story was, because it fits even my physical weaknesses. I have difficulty breathing sometimes because I am so congested. And ever since I was little, my father would ask, "Why are you always clearing your throat?"

My mother would admonish me for making loud gulping sounds when I swallowed liquid. But I couldn't help it! My throat was tight. Also, I got sore throats at least twice every winter, sometimes more.

It seems my throat has always been the center of my physical health issues. I must have associated speaking to getting killed. Once I resolved this issue, I was able to speak, and in fact give talks and lead workshops too. A wonderful side benefit occurred as well. I haven't had a sore throat for years!

Jessica thus resolved her issue by simply telling herself a story about her possible past life. Even if every detail wasn't accurate, her story was close

> Once I resolved this issue, I was able to speak, and in fact give talks and lead workshops too. A wonderful side benefit occurred as well. I haven't had a sore throat for years!

When you feel anything out of the ordinary and have no explanation for it, you may be remembering a past life.

enough to open her to the truth and bring about a resolution. That was the important thing. Jessica was closer to her past than she thought. We all are.

You remember past lives more often than you may think.

When you feel anything out of the ordinary and have no explanation for it, you may be remembering a past life. Fears, phobias, and unexplained beliefs fall into that realm.

The next chapter shows you how you may be able to clear out the clutter of these nuisances through exploring lives past.

3

Resolving Fears, Phobias and Old Beliefs

As we face ourselves, we begin to recognize that a certain thing has held us back from the next step on the path to God. Finally we realize we don't need that particular problem any-more. It's the recognition and the realization of it which allows the karma to be burned off.

— Harold Klemp, *Cloak of Consciousness,*
Mahanta Transcripts, Book 5[1]

People who take the plunge into the past for healing often come up with pearls. The stories in this chapter will show you how people became free from unfounded fears—like a fear of swimming, riding in an airplane, or being in a sailboat; fear of bugs; and more. One person overcame writer's block and another got rid of claustrophobia.

Getting to the root of a past-life issue has often taken me to the root cause of an unexplained fear or phobia. I know I fell off a horse and broke my back in one past life and, even though I love horses, I've been afraid of them in this life.

Another example is from Jan, who has been afraid of water and bridges ever since she can remember. There is no reason in *this* life for her to have these fears. Jan explored her past lives through spiritual exercises like the ones in this book and discovered the cause. She had drowned in a previous life after an accident, when she fell off a bridge. Now she is aware of the reason for her fear and can let it go in her own time.

When a fear, phobia, or belief doesn't match what we have been taught or what we have experienced in this life, you can bet it's from a past life.

THE PROOF IS IN THE RESOLUTION

How can we know for sure if uncomfortable feelings come from a previous lifetime?

There may be no absolute way of knowing your fear stems from a past life; you may only gain a sense that it does. The real proof is in the resolution. You can try to resolve a phobia, belief, fear, or attitude that has been plaguing you by exploring a past life. If you get results, then you know there is some connection.

When I realized I had no basis for my fear of horses in this life, I asked myself what experience from the misty past might have caused the fear.

> saw a man bent over, walking in the rain, supported by a crutch. That man was me. He had fallen off his horse and injured his back. I looked further and saw his love for the horse that walked beside him and his fear of riding it. I knew then I had to let go of that life and let go of the fear.

You can try to resolve a phobia, belief, fear, or attitude that has been plaguing you by exploring a past life. If you get results, then you know there is some connection.

I asked a friend who trained horses to work with me. I wanted to do everything with horses that I possibly could, including brush them and clean their hooves after riding. I did so and made friends with Baron, a horse that could sense my every thought, like many animals do. He knew what I wanted him to do—like walk backward, for example—before I even gave the command. Baron was a dream, helping to heal my fear and let me trust horses again.

We will all have different experiences with fears and phobias from previous lives, if we have any at all. They come in a myriad of styles and colors. This chapter contains just a sampling of past-life experiences which have caused uncomfortable and limiting effects for various people in their present lives.

The following story is from a teenager who is fortunate to remember her past lives easily. At seventeen, Julie had an unfounded fear of snakes. This is what she told me:

> Every time I saw a snake, or even a picture of a snake, I went cold all over, feeling a creepy fear I can't even describe. When I think of an image with that feeling, I remember a scene from a past life in a rocky area of the southwestern United States. I saw a large snake thrashing toward me.
>
> I was backed up against some large rocks. I remember feeling cornered, panicked, with no where to go. The snake bit me, and I died.
>
> Once I knew what caused my fear of snakes in this life, I wasn't as scared of them. Now I know that my past lives are affecting me all the time!

Once I knew what caused my fear of snakes in this life, I wasn't as scared of them. Now I know that my past lives are affecting me all the time!

Since past lives are always affecting us, why not expose the ones causing us fear and anguish in this life?

RESOLVE YOUR GREATEST FEARS THROUGH EXPLORING PAST LIVES

Life can be easier to deal with when you are able to discover the root cause of your fears, like Lauren did in the next story.

Lauren decided to get to the bottom of her claustrophobia. Her story shows how clues from this life can lead to past-life recall. She observed her uncommon fears as she went about her life, then recognized their sources over time. She did this by simply opening herself to the awareness. Lauren was willing to know whatever God wanted her to know about the lifetimes that were the cause of her phobia now.

Here's how Lauren's story unfolded:

> 've always felt very uncomfortable in tight spots—even getting into the backseat of a two-door car or pulling a tight sweater over my head. Three particular events in this life made me wonder whether this feeling came from past-life experiences. Occasions which should have been joyful adventures were stained with seemingly irrational fears.
>
> The first incident occurred when I was twelve years old. I was visiting Australia. As I backed down the ladder into an opal mine, the darkness enveloped me and I felt a stinging heaviness in my body that made it hard to keep descending. I felt a horrific, sad fearfulness, an irrational fear that I'd never see daylight again. Only after

Life can be easier to deal with when you are able to discover the root cause of your fears.

climbing back up and looking around at the vast horizon of the Australian Outback could I bring myself to go back down again into the mine.

Several years later, I visited the Moaning Caverns in the Sierra Nevada Mountains. I walked at the front of our tour group. As we descended the darkening spiral stairs, my whole body resisted as if to say, "No!" I could barely move forward. Again, I was filled with that heavy tingling feeling.

Calming myself, I went to the rear of our tour group where no one could block my exit. As long as I could see an escape route, I was fine. The feeling of having narrowly escaped mortal danger lasted for several hours after I drove away from a seemingly innocuous situation.

On a third occasion in St. Louis, Missouri, my sister and I visited the famous Gateway Arch on the Mississippi River. My sister noticed I became pale and shaky when we began to ascend in a very small elevator. I began to sing HU to calm myself (described on page 13). As long as I could see out of a very small window into the relative openness of the staircase, I was able to keep from panicking.

In each one of these incidents of claustrophobia, I had been able to proceed, but only after doing battle with deep, visceral, and completely irrational fear. I could only wonder where such strong feelings could have originated.

Because I wanted to free myself from these fears and move forward, I looked for deeper causes.

When I started exploring the past-life possibilities, I came up with some bits and pieces that made a pattern.

Because I wanted to free myself from these fears and move forward, I looked for deeper causes. When I started exploring the past-life possibilities, I came up with some bits and pieces that made a pattern.

> Centuries ago, in a small European war, I was hidden in a trunk being smuggled into some kind of large fortress. This journey was of strategic importance to my military unit, as I was to gather vital information and bring it back to my military commanders.

In the first cluster of images, I somehow knew I had been enclosed in a small space on purpose: Centuries ago, in a small European war, I was hidden in a trunk being smuggled into some kind of large fortress. This journey was of strategic importance to my military unit, as I was to gather vital information and bring it back to my military commanders.

A fellow spy, posing as a simple laborer, smuggled me in. Before he could let me out of the trunk, he was caught. He didn't dare say anything about me, and no one else knew I was there. I waited for my release, not knowing my conspirator had been captured. I couldn't move or free myself. Helpless, terrified, and eventually hopeless, I died a painful and very unglamorous death inside the trunk.

I gradually uncovered two more lifetimes involving confinement. The next was very brief: I only remember something being thrown over my head and shoulders so I couldn't see (I had apparently done something very unpopular, and someone felt I needed to learn not to do it again). I realized I was being bagged. Then I was tossed in a river to drown.

In the third lifetime I recalled, I was trapped by accident. While exploring passageways of some natural caverns, I got lost. I felt very disoriented and scared. Desperately trying to find a way out, I crawled into a tight space. It was actually a dead end. The way I had crawled in was fine, but backing out was impossible. Since there was no room to turn around, I was trapped there, overwhelmed with panic, and died of suffocation.

These traumatic experiences led me to associate confinement in close spaces with pain, terror, and death. Death for me was an event charged with powerful emotions and fears.

By looking from the viewpoint of Soul, I was able to separate the fear and pain of the circumstances surrounding the event, from the event itself. Once I saw that the "I" who witnessed these endings did not actually cease to exist—indeed, cannot be killed—I could see that those events were simply doorways between different states or "versions" of being. I have learned that pain may be unpleasant, but is transitory. Whereas the love that fills us—and is our true substance—is everlasting.

SOUL CANNOT BE HURT OR KILLED

Soul (your true self) is eternal, therefore, indestructible. So what is there to fear?

Soul does not fear; only the mind and emotions experience fear. I notice that when I am experiencing life as Soul, I feel no fear.

I've thought about fear a lot, wondering what its purpose might be. I realized fear is necessary to protect the physical body from harm. It's a warning device. However, when we have had too many frights in too many lives, fear can get out of hand and make us withdraw from life.

A seemingly innocent and small fear can affect our lives so much, we don't even realize we're being held back. Emily had this type of phobia. In her present life it kept her from taking on desired projects, being seen in public, and generally enjoying life to

Soul does not fear; only the mind and emotions experience fear.

its fullest. This subtle fear of being noticed finally got Emily's attention. She decided it was time to find its source.

Emily had just begun to explore her past-life possibilities with the issue of this fear. At first she had only a few vague feelings. But with further attention and by examining her dreams, she was able to untangle the root of this problem. She says:

> From the time I was small, I have been overly self-conscious. It got in my way as a child and kept me from being spontaneous. If someone commented on anything I was doing, I didn't want to be noticed. I withdrew.
>
> As I grew up I was OK doing things until I felt that someone noticed. Then I got very uncomfortable. Even now, I still feel this, and it interferes with my spontaneity.
>
> I've had many nightmares of being pursued, and one of the ways I tried to save myself was to not be noticed. I tried to hide, be self-effacing.
>
> In the nightmares people with sinister intent were always chasing me. Sometimes I was trying to protect others and sometimes myself. These pursuers were people with power. They had either physical or political power, but mostly political power—power to sway other people to think ill of me and overlook their evil intentions.
>
> These people were very wealthy, living in a place where others were a drain on their resources. Necessities like food and water were in short supply. It didn't matter to them if others went without. They were plotting to further their own ends and didn't care if they brought damage to the community. They were uncon-

This subtle fear of being noticed finally got Emily's attention. She decided it was time to find its source.

cerned for other people, only wanting safety and gratification for themselves.

I've also had dreams of planes being overhead, flashes of light in the distance, bombs being dropped, and fire all around.

Emily eventually came to the conclusion that she'd been through some kind of war in a past life. There had been some powerful people so concerned for themselves that they took everything they could. To cover themselves, these people blamed innocent citizens for their theft. Emily had been one of those citizens.

Now that she's aware of the roots of her self-consciousness, Emily can work to untangle them.

Do you suspect there are some tangled roots from past lives affecting you? You can try this next exercise to see if there might be a source in some previous life for a present fear.

In order to get to a past-life experience, you can ask yourself questions.

Exploration Exercise: Ask Yourself Questions

1. In order to get to a past-life experience, you can ask yourself questions. If you try this, you may want to write some of these questions down, write the answer, then write down more questions to get deeper, with more details. Try questions like:

   What happened?
   Who was involved?
   Why did it happen?
   Where did it happen?
   How did it happen?

2. If all you can think of is "I don't know," imagine you *do* know. Write a story right from your imagination. It may seem like fiction at first, but as you get into it, it will become very real to you if it is indeed one of your past lives.

Trust your intuition, your inner spiritual guidance, to see if there is a connection between the story and the problem or challenge you are currently facing. You will know if it's real by your own inner perceptions and by looking at how the pieces fall together to make sense of your life now.

Give yourself a few days or weeks to let the idea of this possible past life settle in.

KEEPING YOUR SENSE OF HUMOR HELPS YOU SEE THE PAST

It helps when working with past lives to keep your sense of humor. With some lifetimes, it's possible. My former husband and I used to joke with each other about things we did to each other in previous lives. One of us might say, "You tortured me in a past life!" and the other, "Well, you probably deserved it." Then we'd laugh, knowing those were just roles we played.

A friend, Phil, was able to keep his sense of humor too, even as he felt fear from a past life. He used this fear as a link to carry him into the past and discover its almost humorous, though painful, origin.

Phil had a constant fear of being chased. He felt like everything he did had to be done right now, right

---

Trust your intuition, your inner spiritual guidance, to see if there is a connection between the story and the problem or challenge you are currently facing.

this minute or . . . or . . . or what? Here's the past life Phil recalls:

> *I* was a young boy being chased by a bear. Thinking I would prove myself to be a man, I had gone bear hunting. Now the bear was hunting me!
>
> There was no choice but to jump in the river. This river was at the bottom of a canyon. I was running toward a cliff at the top of this canyon. I thought it would be a clear jump. The only problem was there were some huge boulders between me and the river. I fell right onto the boulders, injuring myself so badly that by the time I hit the river, I was unconscious. I drowned in the river.
>
> This translated into a certain fear in my present life: when I had a project to do, I felt I was being chased. The bigger the project, the more tense I got about getting it done immediately, which was, of course, impossible! I had put myself in a double bind because of this past-life fear.
>
> Now I am calming down and taking things more slowly. I'm enjoying the process more, instead of the result. I know now I won't get killed if I don't get everything done immediately.

Slowing down has been a hard lesson for me this lifetime too, because I had a fear similar to Phil's. This fear was that I was not working fast enough or hard enough. My friends told me I worked harder than anyone they knew, but I didn't believe it. I needed to slow down before I made myself ill. I asked the Mahanta to show me any past life that may shed light on this fear for me. Here is what I was shown:

The bigger the project, the more tense I got about getting it done immediately, which was, of course, impossible! I had put myself in a double bind because of this past-life fear.

I was a large, heavy male, working as a farm laborer. I earned my room and board, but nothing else. I was very slow both mentally and physically. Because I had been born with a mental handicap, I was kept on the farm as a favor to my parents. However, the owners treated me more like a slave.

I saw images of being beaten, especially around my head. This happened more often than not. It was an attempt by my supervisors to get more work out of me. I could only work so fast. I was at my limit. Finally, I got extremely frustrated and anxious about not being able to do what they wanted. I was in pain all the time from being beaten for something over which I had no control. How could I stop the pain? One day, out of hopelessness and anguish I stuck my poor, aching head in the cool river and drowned myself.

After remembering that lifetime, I asked myself what I might have done to have to experience a life of such treatment. I saw an image of myself as a slave master in Egypt, whipping slaves to work harder. I did this because I thought the pharaoh was a god, and this was his edict. Nonetheless, I still needed to see how my thoughtless acts of violence inflicted pain and anguish on another person, a person just like me.

> I still needed to see how my thoughtless acts of violence inflicted pain and anguish on another person, a person just like me.

The memory of the Egyptian life helped me forgive the people I worked for in my lifetime on the farm and also myself for being so imperfect. Once I did this, I was able to begin to slow down. It has taken time, but this new awareness is continuing to help me heal.

Love/Fear Experiences Can Be Explained by Reincarnation

Past-life fears may be confusing because they may be mixed with love. Fears can be confusing when there is a fear of something you *also love*. Past lives pile up, one upon the other, so emotions about the same thing can be mixed. For example, Robin had a love/hate relationship with water:

*M*y love of water was due to spending lifetimes as a pirate or warrior on ships at sea. I had a yearning to join the coast guard when I was younger. I've always loved water and adored sailing, but I was afraid of swimming.

This fear of water surfaced when I was four years old. I was on a large body of water for the first time, crossing on a ferry. I grabbed the center post and hung on for dear life, screaming and crying. I was petrified.

Why was I so scared?

As an adult, I found out why water instilled panic in me. I had drowned in several lives, not just one. I remember waking up in a cold sweat from dreams of being at sea and drowning. The irony is, these were the very lifetimes in which I developed a love for the water as a pirate, warrior, or merchant marine. Either my ship sank or I was killed in the midst of battle or piracy.

I know now there is no great fear that doesn't have a reason. I also know I'm free to let go of these fears from the past, as they no longer serve a purpose but have only held me back. I am beginning to enjoy swimming now, when I go for a sail. Life is becoming bigger and broader with new uncharted territory!

Here's a story that shows the opposite paradox to Robin's, where he loved sailing yet feared swimming. Ashley adored swimming, but sailing was her nemesis:

> loved swimming, the ocean, and rowboats, but I hated sailboats! This simply didn't make sense until I discovered past lives can affect this one.
>
> In one lifetime I was working on a fishing boat. A storm came upon us and I lost my life. In another life I was kidnapped from an island, also in a sailboat. Since the fear is from a past life, I can understand it better now, even if it doesn't completely disappear.

It's amazing how many opposite emotions can pull at us from our former lives and buried images. What a relief to find out we're not crazy, just reincarnated!

Like those in the two previous past-life stories, a good friend of mine had a love/fear relationship. His involved flying. He tells this story to explain it:

> 've gone through cycles of both loving and hating flying. Now I love to fly in airplanes, but until recently, I still had a slight fear about it.
>
> When I was younger, my father took us on flights all over the country. The flights were free; he was an employee of a major airline. Even though I was a little scared, I was fairly quiet until we got in a propeller-driven airplane.

It's amazing how many opposite emotions can pull at us from our former lives and buried images. What a relief to find out we're not crazy, just reincarnated!

Then I started howling and screaming. My father remembers distinctly it was only this type of airplane that threw me into fits.

After I grew older and studied past lives, I remembered one in which I was a World War II pilot. We were on a mission in central Europe. I heard antiaircraft artillery exploding around me. My airplane, a prop plane, crashed, and I died. That was the type of airplane I feared as a child in this life.

The fear from my past life slowly dissipated with continued awareness and letting go of the old images. It helped for me to breathe deeply and surrender to God whenever the fear came up when I flew. I would then tell myself that the old images were from the past, saying to myself, "That was then, this is now." Now I can fly and feel just fine.

YOU CAN SEE THE ILLUSION OF FEAR WHEN LOOKING FROM THE SOUL VIEWPOINT

If we are avoiding relatively harmless situations due to an overriding fear, then it may also be a past-life intrusion, like it was for George in the next story.

George decided to look from a higher viewpoint to see why being overcautious prevented him from enjoying nature as much as he'd like. Caution can be useful when it protects us. But we can go overboard when it interferes with enjoying life fully. What happened to George?

Caution can be useful when it protects us. But we can go overboard when it interferes with enjoying life fully.

I have an inordinate fear of some bugs, especially ticks. I identified the cause through past-life exploration. One lifetime was in Africa during a famine. Everyone was quite ill, and we were in some kind of prison camp. The bugs feasted on us, and many of us died a slow, miserable death.

The next relevant lifetime I saw was one in which I died from Rocky Mountain spotted fever due to a tick bite. I was on my way from the eastern United States to California during the gold rush. I was an ambitious young man with ideas and potential. Having achieved some measure of success in life, I already had a lot going for me. It was so frustrating that I never got to finish the journey and find my gold!

It may be interesting to note that in this life I was born in the foothills of the Rockies. Then my family moved to San Francisco, the destination in my previous life.

Also, I had fevers until I was in high school. The doctors could find no explanation for the fevers. When I was in junior high school, I got bitten by a tick and had to have it removed from my neck. So much distress and fear surfaced then. I work constantly to let it go, even though it still plagues me at times.

When old fears and anxieties from previous lives surface, they sometimes lessen over time if we can be aware that they are dead images from the past. If they get stuck, you can be sure they are illusions hanging on like a sticky residue that needs the oil of Holy Spirit to loosen it. Getting above the problem, viewing it from the highest viewpoint, that of Soul, helps us understand the illusory nature of old fears.

Here's a technique that has helped me to let go of past-life fears: When I feel fear surfacing that I

> When old fears and anxieties from previous lives surface, they sometimes lessen over time if we can be aware that they are dead images from the past.

suspect is from a past life, first of all I make sure I'm breathing deeply! Next, I tell myself the fear is attached to something that is now dead and gone, and it has no power over me unless I allow it. I decide that I will take charge and change the channel as if I were watching television. Changing the channel simply means that I shift my attention from the fear to love by looking at something higher, brighter, and happier.

The easiest way I know to do this is to sing HU, as given in a previous exercise on page 13. It's very calming and uplifting, allowing me to see from the Soul viewpoint and know that everything in this moment is just fine as it should be.

Fear comes in many forms and can sneak into even the most innocuous situations. This next story shows how the thought of a new career or enhancing a present career with a new skill can pull up ancient terrors. Terry tells us about his experience with this:

> Changing the channel simply means that I shift my attention from the fear to love by looking at something higher, brighter, and happier.

My fear of writing has held me back in this life. In my career in health, I could help so many people by putting my research into writing. But I've been afraid. I wanted to get to the bottom of this fear, so I asked to be shown its root cause.

One night I remembered three lifetimes in one dream. In the first, I was walking quickly down a narrow hallway, trying hard not to attract attention. I hoped no one would stop and ask what I had in my leather satchel. It was a dreary time in history; church and state were united. I had been writing essays describing this situation as power out of control, signing them "The Hound." I knew I could be hanged if I were caught.

In the next scene I was leaning over a table, writing by dim candlelight. This was a different lifetime in which I was bold enough to be helping others translate the Bible into English. My work had to be done in secret since there were groups who would kill me if they caught wind of my nightly ritual.

In a third lifetime, I was an English attorney. Once again, I was wary of anyone who knew what I might be writing. I was defending the peasants with my writing, warning them about how the law really worked.

When I awoke from this dream in a sweat, I knew exactly where my fear of writing had come from. It began to dissipate. I began writing more in my business and even completed a manual about health! The fear that followed me from the past is gone now, and I feel free.

> When I awoke from this dream in a sweat, I knew exactly where my fear of writing had come from. It began to dissipate.

FEARS CAUSED BY A PAST LIFE ARE OFTEN FEARS WE CAUSED OURSELVES

I've broken the laws of family, nation, and God in many past lives and caused my own pain, grief, and fear. The next story of fear is from my own life:

From the time I was on my own, I paid my bills as soon as they arrived, before I even knew whether I would have grocery money left!

I hated owing people money, even my mother. I rarely borrowed.

As careful as I was about paying my debts, I soon found myself in a tight financial bind. I had to call my creditors to make arrangements to pay them more slowly. This caused such fear in me I couldn't believe it. There was no basis for it that I knew of in this life. I decided it was time to look into the past.

As I was sitting at my desk, looking at my pile of bills, the images unfolded. I was in a female body, dressed in rags, surrounded by brick walls. I was crying and clawing at the bricks, trying to find a way to escape. Our family had not been able to pay our debts, so here I was in debtor's prison. The fear and anguish overwhelmed me. What would happen to my family? What would happen to me?

Once I became aware of the source of my fear, I took steps to resolve it by letting go of the emotion. I made a promise to myself to think positively about my finances and let go of worry. It has taken some time and inner discipline, but my life is so much easier now.

Years later, my debts began piling up again. Even though I was no longer panicked about them, I looked back further:

I was the minor monarch of an insignificant little village. When my subjects owed me taxes, I used every means to get them paid. I set up delinquent taxpayers as an example and used physical violence to make others fear for their lives if they did not pay their taxes.

It was hard for me to admit the memory of that life into my conscious mind. I was surprised that I could ever have been so cruel to people. And so I

I made a promise to myself to think positively about my finances and let go of worry. It has taken some time and inner discipline, but my life is so much easier now.

learned that judgment of others becomes ludicrous when I look at life from the viewpoint of a well-experienced Soul.

KARMA IS SIMPLY A GOOD TEACHER; GUILT IS UNNECESSARY

We have created situations in this life to learn lessons from mistakes made in other lives. Put simply, we learn from our karma. I used to think of karma as punishment, but I have come to realize it's simply a good teacher, completely neutral. When I think of it this way, I feel more free. Harold Klemp puts it another way:

> *Divine Spirit will help you in the direction you need for your unfoldment. But when things do go wrong, as they will, don't say, "God has forsaken me." Rather say, "God loves me so much that He's giving me the opportunity to learn this about myself, to learn how to become a more spiritual being."*[2]

Guilt can cause more problems than it solves. Here are some past-life experiences that created guilt in this life.

Marissa decided she'd had enough of guilt. How could she resolve this awful feeling that came up during the most minor faux pas? She solved the mystery when she came across a past life while musing on her feelings of guilt:

One of my past lives was as a submarine officer in World War II. I was Japanese. I remember the submarine sinking because of a

Put simply, we learn from our karma. I used to think of karma as punishment, but I have come to realize it's simply a good teacher, completely neutral.

bad decision on someone's part. Then I saw an image of a group of us making the decision, but for some reason, I felt the full impact of the responsibility for it. I remember, as the submarine and all the men aboard were demolished, thinking I could have done better. However, I was somehow able to forgive myself. The lesson in that life was to learn to let go of guilt and move on.

Arlene also had feelings of guilt. "Whatever I do," she said, "I always feel it's not enough. I feel as though I can never do anything right!"

When Arlene considered the possibility of a past life influence, she got the following insight.

> I see an image of a young woman who didn't listen to her father. He warned her an invasion was coming and said she should take measures to protect herself and her son. She was headstrong and didn't listen. Both she and her son were taken away to slavery. Her father was killed.
>
> I was the young woman in that life. I know now that my feelings of guilt and inadequacy were certainly strengthened in that life, if not created then. Now I have to let go of the feelings of guilt, in order to heal completely.

Strong feelings of guilt can also come from old beliefs, often religious. Cameron has one such past-life belief affecting her in this life:

> I never broke my vow of poverty taken in a past life as a monk. This lifetime I find it difficult to earn a good income and maintain my view of myself as a spiritual person. The two do

Strong feelings of guilt can also come from old beliefs, often religious.

not seem to mix in my mind! I feel guilty about being wealthy and believe that being rich is not spiritual and I am taking my attention off God.

However, when I look around me, I see very spiritual, wealthy, good-hearted people serving God. I am working at seeing myself this way too. Now I know that serving God is not about poverty, but about giving from what I have to give. If I have more, I can give more.

Would you like to clear some past-life fears or beliefs that may be affecting this life? The next exercise may help.

> Now I know that serving God is not about poverty, but about giving from what I have to give. If I have more, I can give more.

Exploration Exercise: A Letter to God

1. Relax in a quiet place where you will not be disturbed for about twenty minutes.

2. Think about a fear, phobia, feeling of guilt, or old belief plaguing you in this life. Write in your journal something like this: *Dear God* (or *Dear Mahanta*), *please give me the answer to this problem.*

3. Sing the word *HU*, introduced in chapter 1. It's pronounced like the word *hue* and sung in a long drawn-out breath.

   Sing HU for as long as you are comfortable doing so, up to twenty minutes.

4. Allow any images to come to mind, writing them down as you remember them. Trust that you will know what they relate to.

If they are not clear for you, ask God to help you see the answers more clearly. Allow some time, and consider repeating the exercise daily for at least two weeks. Each time you do the exercise, see if a few more details surface and write them in your journal.

WHAT IF YOU DON'T REMEMBER ANY PAST LIVES?

Now that you've read about past lives in this book, some past-life images may be starting to surface. But what if you don't see, hear, or feel anything?

Can you still work with past lives?

Yes!

Any fears, phobias, unwanted old attitudes, deep frustrations, anxiety, pain, or any other emotional, mental or physical issues can be worked out here and now, even if they're from past lives you don't remember. Jake did this and wasn't aware of a past life until afterward:

When I was younger I was very scared of some dogs, especially large ones. The small ones would nip at my heels. But even though they had never bitten me, larger dogs frightened me more. I knew there must be a reason for this but didn't know where to find it. So I asked my inner spiritual guide, the Mahanta, for help. It came in the form of my brother.

My brother was a dog trainer, so he helped me get over my fear. One day he brought two of his guard dogs over. One Doberman was in

Any fears, phobias, unwanted old attitudes, deep frustrations, anxiety, pain, or any other emotional, mental or physical issues can be worked out here and now, even if they're from past lives you don't remember.

the house with us and started to jump on me. I was really scared, but my brother said, "Just smack him gently on the side of his head and tell him to stay down." I couldn't believe he told me to do that! I was afraid, but I tried it each time the dog jumped on me, being careful to never hurt the dog. By the third time, the dog stayed down! I couldn't believe it.

I overcame this fear and learned to talk with many different dogs in a commanding voice. And they would respond.

Later, when someone asked me about it, I wondered where all this fear had come from. I immediately saw an image of myself in a past life, in the woods with a pack of large wild dogs. They surrounded me, as wild dogs do with their prey. I froze in my tracks, not able to do anything else. I did not survive. The pack tore me to pieces.

I overcame this fear from a past life without having to first remember the past life! It was because I knew I had the loving protection of my inner spiritual guide and the determination to overcome my fear. I was so tired of being afraid and decided I just wasn't going to be that way anymore! I learned that conquering any kind of fear for me is just learning that I don't have to accept it. If I don't accept it, it doesn't scare me anymore.

> I learned that conquering any kind of fear for me is just learning that I don't have to accept it. If I don't accept it, it doesn't scare me anymore.

You can use Jake's technique to ask for help from the spiritual guide you look to. If you don't have one, ask the Mahanta. He is here to help any Soul who asks. Just say, "Please help me, Mahanta," or something like that. The words don't matter, it's what's in your heart.

The effort to resolve past-life fears and phobias can bring great gifts of awareness. It can bring consciousness of life as a continuation of events and lessons that build upon each other, creating who we are now. We are, right now, the best we've ever been. Relationships can make us even better, if we tap their potential lessons. They are so rich with experience from past lives that two chapters will be devoted to them.

Some of the most confusing relationships are romances. Talk about fear! A love interest can keep a person wondering if they're going to come out of the experience in one piece! We'll explore the past-life impact on several romantic relationships in the next chapter.

> We are, right now, the best we've ever been.

4

Meeting Your Past in Romantic Relationships

*At some point we learn to be gracious enough
to accept responsibility for what goes wrong in
our life. We know that we did the best we could
at that time. And when we can allow others this
same charity as we allow ourselves, then we
have come a long way on the spiritual path.*

— Harold Klemp, *The Eternal Dreamer,*
Mahanta Transcripts, Book 7[1]

Karma plays an
important part
in relationships.
We meet our
past-life
buddies or
adversaries to
learn more
together and
balance the
scales of life.

Karma plays an important part in relationships.
We meet our past-life buddies or adversaries
to learn more together and balance the scales of life.
Harold Klemp describes falling in love like this:

*They fall in love, and they fall into karma.
Two people recognize each other from their
mutual past, and they have something to work
out. There is a very strong attraction between
them. So they work out their karma through the
ways society has approved of: marriage or a
relationship or something like that.*

When two people fall in love, I see two Souls on the journey to truth unconsciously doing what they need to do to balance their own books of life, to balance the scales with each other. Sometime in the past, their balance sheets became full of either too many pluses or too many minuses. They've got to get together to balance the books just a little bit.[2]

> Romantic relationships are so charged with emotion that the memories and lessons stay with us longer. They're such a great tool for spiritual unfoldment.

Romantic relationships are so charged with emotion that the memories and lessons stay with us longer. They're such a great tool for spiritual unfoldment.

If there is a very strong, magnetic, mutual attraction, the karma may be strong as well. The Holy Spirit gives both people the opportunity to balance the scales, fulfill old promises, or learn necessary lessons.

At times the lessons may be very confusing. Angela is in a marriage that was once very difficult, leaving her completely befuddled until she discovered the past-life connection:

*W*hen I met my husband there was a very strong attraction between us, and there still is, but there have been times we've wanted to kill each other! When I explored some past-life memories, I found we actually *had* killed each other.

In one lifetime I recalled, my husband then (who is also my husband now) was yelling at me in an Irish brogue to get into the canning shed with the children. We were at war and battleships were coming very close to the shoreline where we lived. I yelled back at him that I didn't want to go in there. We argued for a long time until he finally pushed me and the children into the shed near our house. He and some other men kept watch in the main house. They remained safe in the house, but the children and I were killed when the shed took a direct hit from a cannon. I carried the feeling of blaming him into this life.

When I looked further, I discovered why he may have unconsciously set up my demise in that life. In a different lifetime I was his younger brother, the third of three sons. My husband in my present life was the eldest brother in the past life, the only one to inherit our family fortune. Being self-absorbed and wily in that life, I decided to have my older brother (the first son) killed after the second son became ill and died. After all, why shouldn't I receive the family fortune, now that one brother was out of the way?

The life where I died in the canning shed was a direct karmic payback.

The basic lesson I learned and keep learning is that love heals all wounds, whether past or present. Love coupled with forgiveness eases the bitter sting of anger. Then a detachment unfolds from having a more expanded viewpoint.

MILK EVERY SITUATION FOR WHATEVER YOU CAN GAIN SPIRITUALLY

When there is karma involved, you can be sure there is a storehouse of lessons. How much would you like to learn from each experience?

Why not milk every situation for whatever you can get spiritually?

When there is karma involved, you can be sure there is a storehouse of lessons. How much would you like to learn from each experience?

It's helped me tremendously to take this viewpoint. It sure beats the alternatives of self-pity or blaming others. Looking at what we can learn for ourselves, we free ourselves from poor attitudes and fly higher spiritually.

For example, many of us have experienced a deep love and attraction for someone we cannot be with, for one reason or another. What could the lesson be? The explanations are different for each situation. Here's Jonathan's:

> *I* was drawn to a woman nine or ten years older than me. We tried to hold back and keep a distance due to our age difference, but we had a strong attraction. I knew it was from a past life. I knew things about her without her having to tell me. Even though we tried to stay apart, a relationship flared up between us, and it burned out just as quickly.
>
> In a past life we had been married and had a child together that died. We even talked about having a child in this life. I believe it was due to the loss of the child in our former life together. However, we were not meant to be together in this life, but we were able to heal the pain of that former life with love, by staying friends and supporting each other.
>
> The worst of the pain came to me when I felt all alone. I had no one I felt I could turn to. I finally surrendered to God and realized then that I was never really alone, because I had the Mahanta, my inner guide. I filled myself with his love.
>
> The experience was not over. I knew somehow that I still had to be there for this dear

Many of us have experienced a deep love and attraction for someone we cannot be with, for one reason or another. What could the lesson be?

friend over the next few years, to help her through other situations, even other relationships. Every time we saw each other, the pain lessened for both of us, perhaps sooner for her. I learned to give her love unconditionally. Finally, I was able to let go completely, then move on, learning that divine love heals all.

Sarah's situation, below, resembled Jonathan's in its tone. A bond of love existed between her and Brent, and it was worked out in their marriage:

> I couldn't believe how strong my attraction for Brent was when we began to date. It was as if a powerful magnetic force, the most powerful you can imagine, was pulling us together. It seemed we had no say in the matter, it was that strong! I wondered why, but didn't fight it. It felt good, like being in love in the most powerful way. There was a strong bond between us, but I found out later it wasn't all love.
>
> As we began to get closer, and more so after we married, Brent became more and more angry and insolent. I was mystified and very hurt. I began to feel disdain for this man I also loved.
>
> What was going on here?
>
> I did a spiritual exercise to get my answer, singing HU and asking the Mahanta for guidance.
>
> I was given an insight during that spiritual exercise. I was shown a past life where I had been an indentured servant who was beaten by her master. The master then was my husband now, whose basic nature is gentle. He would never hit me in this life.

I learned to give her love unconditionally. Finally, I was able to let go completely, then move on, learning that divine love heals all.

I started talking to Brent about the lifetime I remembered, and he then told me about the ones he remembered, where I had been cruel to him. It took us a few years of really listening to each other and being good friends to work out all of the karma, but we did it.

We realized our joining in this life was to forgive each other for past hurts. We eventually remembered we had had pleasant lives together as well, which had provided the love bond to help us through this rough time.

I had no idea such a strong bond could be created by karma. I certainly found out the hard way, and I'm also grateful for the lessons I learned.

DIVINE LOVE IS FOREVER; FEAR IS A TEMPORARY ILLUSION

Divine love is forever. We can always be close to those we love as Soul.

Fear is a temporary illusion, but it can be used as a key to reveal past lives affecting this one. If they are unresolved, past-life emotions don't just dry up and blow away. Paying attention to unresolved fears steers us toward healing and greater spiritual growth.

Paying attention to unresolved fears steers us toward healing and greater spiritual growth.

Being aware of an emotional stir was a gift of healing for Pamela. She had an unusual fear surrounding her new marriage, and she resolved it by exploring her past lives.

Marco and I had only seen each other twice before I knew we were right for each other. There was a lot of love between us.

I was working at a clothing store when Marco

and I met. He would visit me during my dinner breaks. It was his way of letting me know he was interested in me, and the feeling was mutual! I loved him from the first moment I saw him and even more the next! Even though I had never in this life been afraid anyone would leave me, I had an inordinate fear of Marco leaving me once we were together. This made no sense to me, since I was usually the one to leave a relationship.

I asked my inner spiritual guide, the Mahanta, for help. I remembered, with extreme clarity, two lifetimes Marco and I shared, which explained both our great love for each other and my fear.

One night I saw Marco walk into the store and come down a long aisle. As he walked toward me, I admired his jacket—a classic western buckskin with fringe running down the arms. When he reached me, I asked him, "Where is your jacket?" for it had simply vanished. He looked puzzled and told me he had not worn a jacket into the store.

As we ate dinner, Marco related a dream he'd had prior to meeting me. It was clear from the dream that the buckskin jacket was a clue to how we'd known each other before.

In his dream, Marco was a frontiersman who was dying from a gunshot wound fired by an Indian's rifle. He was on the ground being held by a brother who comforted him as his life slipped away. Both men wore buckskin clothing. Marco told me he knew this man was his brother. "Perhaps he was not *biologically* my brother, but he was absolutely my brother *spiritually*," he said.

> I asked my inner spiritual guide, the Mahanta, for help. I remembered, with extreme clarity, two lifetimes Marco and I shared, which explained both our great love for each other and my fear.

I knew that the brother had been me. This made it easy to understand why we shared such an immediate and deep love for one another.

Marco also left me in a lifetime previous to that one, but not by death. We'd been born into different social classes in the Victorian era. I could see the scenes in that life with utter clarity in a dream I had. He was a celebrated playwright born to a very wealthy family. I was from a nondescript family, possessing only the advantage of physical beauty. I adored him.

Observing both of us in this dream, I understood he had been fond of me and enjoyed my admiration. But I could also see the darker side of this friendship. He and his higher-class peers regarded me as an amusement, because of my puppylike devotion.

In that lifetime, Marco's plays and writing were his true loves. He thrived on surrounding himself with admirers, using this energy to achieve his success.

My dream continued, showing me the day I decided to profess my love to Marco. We were in the great kitchen of his mother's mansion. His mother and her kitchen maid returned from their shopping, surprising us in the middle of an amorous encounter.

Shocked (and frightened of his domineering mother), Marco bolted from the kitchen, leaving me alone and mortified.

Now my dream showed us both about twenty years later. I was standing at the black wrought-iron gate of a cathedral. A wedding procession was leaving the church, and Marco was the last in line. This was his daughter's wedding day. I

> Observing both of us in this dream, I understood he had been fond of me and enjoyed my admiration. But I could also see the darker side of this friendship.

saw him, but he did not see me. His face was not lit with joy as one would expect on such an occasion; it had the look of one serenely resigned to sadness.

My heart ached as I watched him pass by, for all those years later I was still deeply in love with him.

I learned from that life not to give my power away to another individual by creating my whole world around them. Now God is central in my life, and my family is part of that.

Pamela said that her previous lives with Marco were heartbreaks that turned into heart openings and highlighted the importance of God for her in this life. She said her heart is more open to all life now and her fear of Marco leaving her is gone.

GRATITUDE FOR THE OPPORTUNITY TO WORK OUT PAST-LIFE KARMA MOVES US FORWARD

Elizabeth's heartbreak, described below, turned into a heart opening as well:

*M*y husband had an affair in this lifetime with someone he felt very connected with due to their common interest in music. I felt such rage; I couldn't believe it. In the meantime, he didn't know whether to stay or go and seemed afraid to leave. He was actually afraid of me! I had to look at this from another perspective. What was going on?

I explored the possibility of other lives. What came to me was an image of the very same setup. I had been married to him in another life, but I was a man then and he was my wife. We

> I learned from that life not to give my power away to another individual by creating my whole world around them. Now God is central in my life, and my family is part of that.

were both from wealthy families, and my wife had brought shame upon us by having an affair. I flew into a rage and accidentally killed her.

After that memory, I knew why I was in a rage and why my husband was afraid of me and afraid to leave. He had repeated the same old scenario and expected me to do the same. I did not, however, since I knew better in this life. I gave him the freedom of choice and let him go, trying to understand his feelings and staying friends.

Soon after, I met the man of my dreams, and we are a better match than my first marriage.

I was rewarded for my patience and understanding in this life. I can see how much I grew spiritually in between lifetimes and how just giving love heals all.

Exploring how we've caused our own grief in every situation is a great challenge at times, even though Elizabeth made it sound easy. Though her heart hurt terribly, she moved beyond herself to see how she had set up her own difficulties.

Heartbreaks don't just come from relationships. Lack of a romantic relationship can be almost as painful as having one in which your heart is broken. This solo experience can also be mined for gems of great spiritual value. Michelle decided to escape from self-pity by exploring the cause of her present-day loneliness.

> Lack of a romantic relationship can be almost as painful as having one in which your heart is broken. This solo experience can also be mined for gems of great spiritual value.

*E*very relationship I've had with a man has failed. I've often thought I wasn't meant to be married in this lifetime, attributing it to karma earned in other lives.

To be happier, I focus on being grateful for the privilege of working off karma in this lifetime. I'm trying hard not to feel the sense of deprivation and stay focused on the gift. When I do this, I get more insight as well.

When I thought about a possible past-life connection to my present situation, I began to feel a sense of loss and abandonment. Several images came to mind. At first they were just feelings. I allowed them to come up and watched the images emerging from the feelings.

There was a feeling of someone being taken away from me. It was not my choice, or the choice of the one being taken. They were removed by force.

Next, I felt the situation unfold in myself. I began to see that I was a young slave woman whose husband was taken away. I see him looking at me with despair, trying to reach out to me. There's nothing either of us can do.

Then, I remember just going on in despair. I think I had a small child. I gave too much attention to my heartache and not enough to the child. I got caught up in the tragedy of not having my husband in my life and neglected my child as a result.

I learned from that life to take full responsibility for a partnership and family, including children. That also meant loving them fully and helping them grow toward their own unfoldment. It's taken me a long time this lifetime to address the issue of responsibility. I've taken it on, but it's always been a scary prospect, especially failing. Somehow I knew that disastrous results would occur if I did.

I learned from that life to take full responsibility for a partnership and family, including children. That also meant loving them fully and helping them grow toward their own unfoldment.

Michelle told me she knew that in that tragic lifetime she was reaping the karmic return for a previous life. She shared her story with me.

I was a wealthy young woman, quite spoiled. My wealth must not have been enough for me because I stole my brother's inheritance. I was also very much of a flirt.

I was very irresponsible about my relationships with men and probably broke a lot of hearts. Getting into relationships for me was fun, nothing serious, and I thought my suitors shouldn't have taken them seriously either.

I always had my way, even as I got older, because I had money to influence people, and I thought this was my right. Later, as I aged, I thought about how I might have hurt people in ways I never understood at the time. Eventually, I became a bitter old woman and was very much alone toward the end of my life.

As I reflected on life at the end, I knew I needed to learn an important lesson. This was to love and act responsibly in any relationship— to be a true partner. I learned the value of contributing to the other person's happiness and unfoldment as well.

GOD BECOMES THE CENTER AFTER REMOVING THORNS FROM PAST LIVES

Michelle's attitude of being grateful for the opportunity to work out past-life karma is commendable. Loneliness can indeed be heartbreaking. Yet, the heart may often break open. Sometimes there's no other way to make room for the greater love of God.

> I knew I needed to learn an important lesson. This was to love and act responsibly in any relationship—to be a true partner. I learned the value of contributing to the other person's happiness and unfoldment as well.

In reply to a question asked him about love, Harold Klemp says, "There is a lot of pain that goes with love, as you surely know firsthand. But the fire of love brings a change in spiritual outlook that cannot come by a shorter path."[3] Further, in answer to someone in anguish about a relationship spiraling down, Harold Klemp solves the riddle of life for many people by explaining that "The turmoil of lost affection that you are experiencing is actually Soul's desire for God."[4]

Learning how to open the heart to greater love is why we're here on earth and why we go through such difficulties.

Shirley had an experience from a past life seep into this life to drive her toward opening her heart to herself and to God's love for her. She has never felt she was pretty or attractive. Were her feelings of inadequacy related to something beyond this life? In her words:

> All of my life I have felt unworthy of love. People have always told me I was beautiful, but I never believed it. I know they were seeing something beyond physical beauty, something I couldn't relate to. I felt I wasn't worthy of anyone's love and certainly not God's. I knew I had to learn to rely on myself for assurance and a strong sense of self-worth, but how?
>
> Recalling one past life left me in tears, it touched me so deeply. This began the healing process. In that lifetime I was born into a wealthy family, a daughter of a highly successful merchant. At age seventeen, I was being courted by a minor lord. He was only interested in my

Learning how to open the heart to greater love is why we're here on earth and why we go through such difficulties.

money, for I was no great beauty nor was I witty.

My father observed this man and came to the conclusion he would only hurt me. Yes, he would marry me. But once he had my dowry and inheritance, he would easily abuse my love. In order to protect me, my father spoke to this lord without my knowledge. Father told the man that he would not approve the marriage.

The dismissed lord was very angry. He came to me and said, "You are so ugly that no one could ever love you or want you!"

Because I had no idea my father had spoken to this man, I thought this was his true feeling. I couldn't figure out what had happened, why he no longer wanted to marry me. I was so distraught that I killed myself.

The pain of that rejection carried into my present incarnation. At seventeen in my present life, still feeling ugly, unloved, and unhappy, I attempted suicide. As an adult, I looked back upon that attempt at ending my life as a selfish, childish act. I had no idea there was a past-life connection.

I developed the quality of fierce independence in this life, with a strong mind and body to counteract my previous emotional dependence. Now that I've remembered this past life, I have begun to heal. I am getting more in touch with my heart and forming bonds of love I now know are real.

And a vital realization came to me. I have to be able to love myself, to rely on myself for that love, in order to accept anyone else's love, especially God's!

> I have to be able to love myself, to rely on myself for that love, in order to accept anyone else's love, especially God's!

An opposite situation to Shirley's occurred with Adam. As a woman in a past life, he was not rejected but rejected someone else.

I was the daughter of a landowner in Europe at a time when land was the most important possession. My father had arranged a marriage for me with another landowner, to maintain our family's social and financial standing.

I, on the other hand, wanted no part of it. I would not even meet the landowner to whom I was betrothed. There was no way I would marry someone unknown to me. More important, I was in love with a craftsman in town, and that was who I decided to marry, against my father's orders. My father told me I would not get a dowry of land from him if I married the craftsman.

Even though I married against my father's decision, I thought, out of love, he would at least give us some money. He gave us nothing. I was angry, but I was also in love. I had a happy life despite my father's grievance with me and mine with him. I always resented my father's cold-hearted denial of even a small dowry to help us get started.

Even though I had a good life, one thing got in the way at times. The landowner I had refused to meet frequented our shop. He was actually quite nice and not at all bad to look at. I would have been wealthy, had I married him. I saw what I had rejected, what I lost. This haunted me at times and reminded me of my resentment toward my father.

Even though I had a good life, one thing got in the way at times.

This lifetime I met my rejected betrothed again, as a woman. I was attracted to her, but she rejected my overtures. I learned a lesson. What goes around, comes around. I could see the karma coming back so clearly. I learned something even more important and that was to let go of resentment.

Adam's lesson was quite clear to him. Other lessons can take more time to understand. When they are unraveled, they sometimes reveal the very thread that will heal.

Soul Knows How to Love Unconditionally

Unconditional love comes from God. When someone gives to another, even in the smallest way, without expecting a return, it is unconditional love. God's love comes through us, as Soul, to others and through others to us.

Zachary had an experience of unconditional love healing old wounds. Here's the story of his brief interlude in this life with a spouse from a former life:

I just broke up with someone very special to me. When we first fell in love, I thought she was the love of my life. Our breakup seemed heartbreaking to others who sensed our strong bond with each other. To us, it had become natural and right to go on with our lives as we had before we met. This attitude was highly unusual for me!

After meeting on the Internet through a mutual friend, we met each other physically at a national event we both decided to attend. There

Unconditional love comes from God. When someone gives to another, even in the smallest way, without expecting a return, it is unconditional love. God's love comes through us, as Soul, to others and through others to us.

was no immediate attraction between us. As we got to know each other, however, there was more. I finally decided to visit her in Mexico, where she lived. One evening we went to a dance together, and I knew then that I loved her.

The next morning I woke up with a smile on my face and these words in my head, "It's so nice we're not trying to kill each other." I immediately knew those words referred to a past life we had lived together in fourteenth-century Ireland.

We were married then, and our Irish tempers often got the best of us. Sometimes it was love, sometimes hate. This explained why in this life I was not attracted to her right off. Now we had a chance to enjoy each other's company, with the Irish madness behind us. We really fell in love this time.

Deciding it was best for me to make the move from the U.S. to Mexico, I readied myself as best I could. Job, home, friends, and volunteer work were all reorganized or delegated. However, some of my commitments would take up to nine months to complete. She couldn't take the wait. It was hard on her, not being able to see me very often, and she was quite lonely. Something inside told her this would not work for her, so she broke it off.

We visited each other one more time, because she changed her mind, but then she decided it still would not work for her. Most people in my position would be very frustrated at this point.

The amazing thing about this whole experience is, I not only wasn't angry, I was fine! This never happened to me or anyone else I knew. She seemed very OK with everything too. We

I woke up with a smile on my face and these words in my head, "It's so nice we're not trying to kill each other." I immediately knew those words referred to a past life we had lived together in fourteenth-century Ireland.

both found a place in our hearts where we could love, and we didn't need anything back. And to this day we are still friends and keep in touch.

One of the keys for us was forgiveness. We formally forgave each other for whatever we did or didn't do in the past that may have caused each other unnecessary pain or suffering.

I discovered something heartening from that experience. When the karma is finished, there is only love: love to give and receive. This love, however, is truly unconditional. There are no emotional strings attached.

Zachary revealed an admirable quality: the ability to see beyond the conventional view of love to the higher viewpoint of Soul.

Leah saw the larger picture as well, once she got through the heartache of her brief rendezvous with David.

I met a man I instantly fell in love with. As we were talking about this unusual attraction, we started speaking at the very same moment. We both said, "Where do I know you from?" and then answered each other almost simultaneously, "We were monks together."

Later, we found out we've both had a fear of public speaking from our monk life, and in this lifetime it was time to express what was in our hearts. In our previous lifetime we had both been killed for expressing our beliefs because they were antithetical to the church, or so it was viewed.

The amazing thing is that we met in this life at a class on public speaking! The love we share

> Zachary revealed an admirable quality: the ability to see beyond the conventional view of love to the higher viewpoint of Soul.

now is due to a bond we forged many lifetimes ago as kindred spirits in a world not to our liking. However, in this life, we could not be together. This was very hard for me to accept because of our great love for each other.

My mind told me we should be together, although God had shown me it was not to be in this life. We had different roads to follow, but we'll always be close in our hearts.

We only needed to help each other move forward on our journeys. Now we've each forged new careers, using our past-life training in speaking as vehicles for loving service, without the old fear.

Is it always necessary to get involved in a relationship to work out past-life karma? Other ways of potentially working out the karma from a past-life relationship are through everyday events, dreams, and spiritual exercises.

Here is one exercise that has worked very well for me. I've used it whenever I found myself attracted to someone, and I wanted to be sure I didn't get involved unless it was necessary.

Sing HU out loud or to yourself for no more than twenty minutes. Ask God or the Mahanta to take you to a higher spiritual awareness, a higher plane.

Exploration Exercise:

Checking It Out from the Higher View

1. Sing HU, the ancient love song to God shared in chapter 1. This will take you to the highest awareness, or level of heaven, you are able to reach right now. Sing HU out loud or to yourself for no more than twenty minutes. Ask God or the

Mahanta to take you to a higher spiritual awareness, a higher plane. There are many levels of heaven, as spoken of in the Bible. The higher the plane you can visit in this spiritual exercise, the more you will know about your present situation.

You can ask to do this in your dreams or in your waking spiritual exercise.

2. As you sing HU, ask God to show you the nature of your new potential relationship.

   • Does it need to be a relationship or just a friendship?

   • Is it a passing fancy, or is there a long-term, solid relationship on the horizon for you?

   • Is there a spiritual lesson that you may see without getting involved?

3. Pay attention to whatever you see or hear, whether in your waking state or dream. Write down anything you experience, no matter how insignificant it may seem to you now. You will eventually understand its meaning.

Repeat the exercise for as many days as you feel necessary.

Karma is created by cause and effect, and we can change the cause through knowledge of some basic laws.

What about avoiding unnecessary karma in the future?

Karma is created by cause and effect, and we can change the cause through knowledge of some basic laws. In his book *Wisdom of the Heart*, Book 2, Harold Klemp gives a good explanation of morals and ethics, and how to avoid creating negative karma:

*A moral law is something society makes
you do if you want to live at peace within that
society. Ethics are the fine shadings: you do the
right thing spiritually, even though you may not
gain from it materially. You may even lose. But
it is the right thing to do; it's the spiritual thing
to do.*[5]

He goes on to explain common law, which was
developed when the common people had no one but
the clergy to turn to for resolving conflict or griev-
ances:

*Common law, or scientific law, had a basic
idea: there exists a higher being, and there exists
from this higher being a fundamental law.
Anybody trying to understand and decide law
in those days was actually trying to divine and
learn, very much like a scientist, the laws of
Spirit. What are the fundamental laws of this
higher being?*[6]

Then he tells us of writer Richard Maybury's
distillation of the basic ideas behind common law
and that anyone can use these two principles at any
time, anywhere, to stay close to the spiritual laws:

*Maybury's two laws are the clearest ex-
ample of how to live cause and effect that I can
give you: (1) Do all you have agreed to do, and
(2) do not encroach on other persons or their
property.*[7]

The simplicity of these laws is elegant, and the
laws are easy to understand. They can keep us from
creating too much negative karma while living here

These laws can
keep us from
creating too
much negative
karma while
living here on
earth, and they
can certainly
help improve
all of our
relationships,
no matter
what kind.

on earth, and they can certainly help improve all of our relationships, no matter what kind.

The following story is about a couple who seems to have only good karma from their past lives.

It's a joy when an old friend can actually spend a lifetime with us. Don and Rebecca were blessed in this way. Sometimes it takes years in this life to become aware of the blessing.

Rebecca and Don grew up in the same town and went to the same high school, but they didn't become close friends until college. Rebecca transferred from her university to the college Don attended. They had mutual friends there, but they were still just good friends.

Finally one day their relationship took a romantic turn. Rebecca knew then and there that this was right. She knew they were meant to be together in a romantic relationship as they had been in another lifetime. Rebecca says:

> It wasn't right for us to be together because other people were involved. I passed the test in our previous life by honoring Don's marriage and my own commitments.

I don't write my dreams down, but I remembered this one so well, I didn't have to! Don was another person and I was another person in this dream. We were at a dance and wanted very much to be together but couldn't, not at this time. It wasn't right for us to be together because other people were involved. It seemed he was married and I was with someone else.

After that dream I realized we could now be together in this life, clean and clear. So we married. After twenty years of marriage, I still feel Don is my closest friend and that we will definitely grow old together.

I passed the test in our previous life by honoring Don's marriage and my own commitments. Even though we had been together in lifetimes before that one, we had to stay on track with God. We had always been together in our most spiritual lifetimes, like the lives we were both Tibetan monks. Now we were able to be married because we had earned the right.

There is a certain wisdom we have as a couple, and we are very focused on spirituality in our lives. That's what brought us together—our higher purpose in life.

Don and Rebecca have a rare gift of true spiritual love and friendship. How can we all attain this state?

Learning to give unconditional love, and taking responsibility for our own lessons rather than blaming others, is a key to any successful relationship, be it in friendship, work, or family situations.

In chapter 5 we will continue examining real-life scenarios of various challenging relationships that began in past lives. We'll see how they were made easier by exploring the past-life connections.

Learning to give unconditional love, and taking responsibility for our own lessons rather than blaming others, is a key to any successful relationship, be it in friendship, work, or family situations.

5

Healing Relationships with Family, Friends, and Coworkers

I think it is very important in this life to learn to love someone more than yourself—whether it's another person or a pet.

And before you can love someone else more than yourself, you begin by first loving yourself. Even Christ said, "Love Thy neighbor as thyself." Right away some people think this means love your neighbor and forget all about yourself.

Loving yourself doesn't mean to have a high, egotistical regard for yourself or go strutting around like some dictator. It means to have respect for yourself as Soul, as a child of God— or as we say in ECK [Eckankar], as a light of God. Because once you recognize yourself as Soul, as one of these beings of God, you've made an important step in your spiritual unfoldment.

The next important step is to know and recognize that other people are also Soul, lights of God.

— Harold Klemp, *The Slow Burning Love of God*, Mahanta Transcripts, Book 13[1]

Once you recognize yourself as Soul, as one of these beings of God, you've made an important step in your spiritual unfoldment.

93

*C*hallenges arise throughout our lives, as we grow up with our schoolmates, live with our families, and work with our coworkers. What role might past lives play in helping us understand and overcome these everyday challenges?

Families are often a focus for emotional and spiritual learning. People actually reincarnate into the same family group over and over again to work out karmic patterns that have repeated over millennia. We love each other deeply, but sometimes we want to scream in frustration, like Julie.

Julie faced a tremendous challenge from the day her son was born. He was unusually difficult and completely disrespectful to her. Was this who he was? Or was she somehow to blame for his behavior?

*T*he problem with my son began day one. When Rick was born, I was so distraught. His eyes seemed full of hatred. How could this be? Newborn babies are supposed to adore their mothers, aren't they? He seemed to want to die, just to get away from me. Having been a premature baby, he was very ill.

Even as a baby, Rick would never eat the food I gave him. He always acted like it was poison.

As Rick grew a little bigger, he became very controlling and bossy. In his social world he was charismatic, attracting friends who looked up to him and respected him. You can imagine how confused I was, until I found the answer in a past life I remembered. It made all of the puzzle pieces fit.

Rick was an emperor in our past life to-

> **P**eople actually reincarnate into the same family group over and over again to work out karmic patterns that have repeated over millennia.

gether, and I was his wife. He had been, in my opinion, a bad ruler—very cruel. For the sake of my people, I betrayed and poisoned him. Of course, he wouldn't trust me again in this life.

Once I had this past-life awareness, I apologized to him for killing him. We actually laughed about it. Now he even eats my food!

I've learned to look at both sides of every situation now. More and more I trust the love of the Mahanta, my spiritual guide, to take me to divine love, to help me work together with other Souls.

In families, and elsewhere, apologies can be very powerful. They certainly were for Julie. Apologizing can be a form of love, even though we may not think of it that way.

LOVE IS THE ULTIMATE HEALER FOR ALL SITUATIONS

How does divine love help us see what's really going on and why we have chosen each situation?

When we react to someone or something in an extreme way—when we get our reactive buttons pushed—we can be sure there is a lesson in it for us. The lesson is actually a gift from God.

When in doubt about how to heal pain from a past life or this life, try love. It's the most healing salve of all. As we love each other more, we learn to love God more, as Harold Klemp says:

When in doubt about how to heal pain from a past life or this life, try love.

> *I believe Soul's lesson here is to learn how to love God through loving first ourselves and then our family.*

I don't know if there's a real cause-and-effect relationship. In other words, do you begin by loving God first, and then you're able to love your family and others in this world? Or do you love others first, and then through loving others, you're then able to love God? I don't know. It may be different for everyone. Maybe it's different at different times.[2]

Lydia had a traumatic experience with a family that wasn't her own, but for whom she worked. Her past-life memories woke her up to how she had caused her own troubles. This is her story:

I have worked with children for most of my life. I love working with children, but many of the adults I worked for have been overbearing taskmasters and at times verbally abusive. I was only being paid to be a nanny, but somehow my employers bullied me into cleaning house as well. I wondered why.

One day I was scrubbing the floor for an employer who had threatened to sue me if anything was not perfect on her white ceramic flooring. This was my last day working for her, and I was being very careful, scrubbing the crevices with a toothbrush on my hands and knees. As I finished working, I found myself in tears, saying silently, "Thank you, God, for letting me get out alive!"

Suddenly I saw an image of myself in a past life as a young girl with a hunchback who was unwanted by her parents. I had run away from home at age seven and was taken in to work in an orphanage where I could earn my food and

Lydia had a traumatic experience with a family that wasn't her own, but for whom she worked. Her past-life memories woke her up to how she had caused her own troubles.

shelter. The woman who ran the orphanage was cruel, yet her husband was kind to me. I was whipped by the woman. The other children were cruel to me as well, teasing me mercilessly.

I wondered what I had done to cause the circumstances in that life.

I soon became aware that I had been a dandy in England, enjoying wealth and prestige, but treating others very poorly, especially children. My servants were hit with my cane whenever they displeased me, and poor children on the street were run over by my carriage at times for my lack of concern. I was completely self-absorbed in that life and had no regard for anyone else, especially children, whom I thought were of no value.

In this life I love children, and as soon as my child was born I had a fierce need to protect him. He has had many accidents in this life. Also in this life I have been a procrastinator, perhaps because I was used to my former life of being served and waited on.

I have forgiven myself for my past-life cavalier attitude and have learned the universe doesn't revolve around me. I am much more compassionate in this life than ever before.

It seems impossible to forgive or express love at times, but we stretch our capacity for love every time we try. Relationships are a great classroom to learn how to give love in every way, under every condition. Doing so brings us closer to God, as Harold Klemp tells us: "The way to God is ever within the heart, within the loving heart."[3]

Relationships are a great classroom to learn how to give love in every way, under every condition.

BEING AWARE OF FAMILY CONNECTIONS SHOWS LIFE IN A NEW LIGHT

Sometimes love takes the form of letting go. Pure, unconditional love is really letting go, letting things be. Just as God gives free will to all Souls, we are challenged to give each other the same freedom.

Letting go of our attachment to our children may be the hardest of all. In Gwen's case, this has been difficult. She was surprised to discover that a past life was influencing her attachment.

Three or four days after my daughter Kirby was born, I was overcome with extreme grief. I began weeping. This continued for an hour straight; I just sat, holding my baby and weeping. I knew at the time that this deep sadness was due to some past-life tragedy, but I wasn't ready to know the details.

I felt very protective of Kirby from day one. As Kirby grew older, I felt I had somehow been responsible for a tragedy we had experienced in a past life by some action or inaction on my part. Perhaps I had let go of Kirby's hand at the wrong time. I only knew I had to be very careful now, very responsible. I felt this responsibility keenly.

When Kirby was eleven she was given the opportunity to travel to France with some relatives. I knew she would be safe with them, so I let her go. At the airport, I was feeling sad and nervous about letting my daughter go for the first time in my life. My nervousness made me fiddle with the pen in my pocket. I kept thinking, *Kirby will be so far away, across the ocean in another country.*

> Sometimes love takes the form of letting go. Pure, unconditional love is really letting go, letting things be.

As I walked away from the airplane, which was taking off, I looked down at my hand. The pen I'd been holding had leaked ink, but not onto my hand. It made marks on my wrist that looked very much like the tattoos from Nazi concentration camps. I knew then with all my being that, as a Jew, I had been separated from my child in Hitler's Germany. We were forced to go to separate concentration camps, and we were killed. Now my overprotective feelings made sense!

Having had that realization of Kirby and my past life, I could stop criticizing myself for being so overprotective. I could begin trusting God.

Something I accepted even more was that, if we've lived before, how can Soul ever die? This deeper understanding helped me know that no matter what may happen to my daughter or any of my loved ones, they are always cared for by God from life to life, even through death of the body. The Souls I know and love will live on—not just in my heart, but in the true reality of God.

> The Souls I know and love will live on—not just in my heart, but in the true reality of God.

Gwen had verification of that past life when she looked at certain circumstances in this one. She says:

> came into this lifetime feeling very insecure. I now know it related to World War II bombings, displacement, and loss of family and home.
>
> I also remember being very shy as a child in this life, refusing to speak about what I thought. I was afraid to attract any attention to myself. I feel it was from being suppressed as a Jew in my former life, when Jews were not allowed to say anything or look at or talk to anyone in public. Even though I grew up in a Catholic household, the Jewish culture was close to my heart.

Gwen's daughter, Kirby, now twelve, remembers being in France during World War II, validating her mother's past-life memory. She has a subtle feeling about that life with her mother:

> *I* related strongly to a book I recently read about a Jewish family hiding in a home during the war. I wanted my mother to read this book for some reason. I kept trying to get her to read it. I realized I was trying to get her to remember that past life.

Staying open to solutions from past-life recalls can help resolve even the most challenging family karma.

Staying open to solutions from past-life recalls can help resolve even the most challenging family karma. In the following story, unusual family karma caused an apparent deadlock in a marriage. Anne's insights resolved this seemingly impossible situation. She was given insight into her difficulties when she discovered the past-life cause.

> *My* husband and I were having more and more heated discussions about finances and business. They became shouting matches, where I got frustrated and he became very angry. My feelings were hurt by the fact that he focused so much on our lack of money rather than being grateful for what we had. The most painful thought I had was, *He doesn't even seem to care that at least we have each other.*
>
> I kept blaming him in my mind for our financial mess, thinking his negative attitude about himself was causing our state of affairs. He kept putting himself down and claiming nothing would work for him in his career or any career he might choose. I tried to give him

positive feedback about himself, to no avail. There would be very slight progress, then setback after setback.

Finally, I asked God to show me the answer. "Why did this have to happen? What is *my* spiritual lesson here?" I asked.

I listened for an answer. What I got was a vision. It was an image of an older couple in rags, sitting on the side of the road, destitute. They looked European by their clothing, and the time seemed to be the 1700s. I knew instantly the couple was me and my husband in a former life.

We were talking. He said to me, "Well, at least we have each other."

I answered him with a grunt. I was fed up with our life of poverty and the dear price we had paid in debtor's prison. We had lost everything, including knowing the whereabouts of our children.

I had been the one who was ungrateful in that life. Now I was learning how it felt, by being on the other end of ingratitude. My husband had been sweet and gentle in that life, very willing to let the bad experiences go by without holding on to them. I had taught him to be ungrateful and had to live with the results of that.

Now I understand both sides and have gained compassion for my husband's situation in this life. He is coming out of the dark clouds, slowly but surely, and has been able to support both of us since then.

Seeing how I created this situation opened my eyes to being very careful about how I judge anyone, especially those closest to me who seem easiest to judge. I now know that whenever I

Seeing how I created this situation opened my eyes to being very careful about how I judge anyone, especially those closest to me who seem easiest to judge.

don't like the actions of another, I've done it myself, and I have no right to judge others. "Compassion," was the answer to my question What is my spiritual lesson here?

Once we're aware of past-life situations where we were hurt or felt responsible for others' pain, how can we resolve these?

Forgiveness is a form of divine love.

There are several ways we may find to heal—love is often the most powerful. Forgiveness is a form of divine love. By forgiving others or forgiving ourselves, we may be able to inject more divine love into the situation.

Would you like to try this now?

Exploration Exercise:

Forgiving Others for Past Actions

1. Think of the person you want to forgive. Ask that divine love fill your heart as you do this exercise.

2. If you're feeling any anger or animosity about the situation, talk it out with an imaginary replica of the person, as if he were sitting across from you. Ask why the person did what he did. Talk about this until you begin to feel the emotions draining away.

3. Now simply offer forgiveness in whatever way you like. As an example, you can say, "I forgive you. I know you did the best you could at that time. I now release this situation to God."

You may have to forgive yourself as well, to complete the cycle. Try this next exercise to do so.

Exploration Exercise:
Forgiving Yourself for Past Actions

1. Look at yourself as if you were seated in a chair opposite yourself. As if you were an observer, try to view yourself with divine love.

2. Tell yourself how you feel about your past behavior, saying everything you'd like to say, sharing all you feel, and expressing all your expectations.

3. As in the exercise above, forgive yourself (using the same example, if needed): "I forgive you. I know you did the best you could at that time. I now release this situation to God."

Tell yourself how you feel about your past behavior, saying everything you'd like to say, sharing all you feel, and expressing all your expectations.

Watch what happens to relationships when you forgive others *and* yourself. The results can be miraculous when we truly open our hearts to each other.

Maya gives an example of how forgiveness worked to heal anger and pain from her past.

My former husband and I still own a business together. He used to say things that really hurt my feelings. I had been unable to forgive him for his verbal abuse, penny-pinching, and general slovenliness. Since we still worked together this was very difficult. Then I looked at a past life where I had treated him exactly as he was treating me in this lifetime.

After that, I had no problem forgiving him. I realized my karma was returning very neatly.

What occurred then was miraculous. We are now able to work together in our business and maintain a good level of communication, while respecting each other's freedom.

This level of challenge can also come into play with any career or job relationship. And so much growth can come of it as we realize and heal the past. Shannon had to deal with one such work relationship:

> *I* couldn't understand the way I was being treated by someone in upper management at my company. This particular manager, Lisa, seemed almost jealous of me. How could this be, and why?
>
> I had been doing my very best in an unusually difficult situation. I was an assistant to a bipolar (manic-depressive) man who was unable to function normally at work due to complications with his medication. I was doing both my work and his, because I cared about him as a good friend.
>
> When yearly review time came around I expected to get a raise in salary, since I was quite good at my job. Lisa surprised me with her comments. She said my performance had been terrible. I explained my situation as best I could, telling her about Bill's medical problems and how it created much more work for me. Instead of being concerned about Bill or giving me credit for my efforts, she retorted, "It's your problem,

What occurred then was miraculous. We are now able to work together in our business and maintain a good level of communication, while respecting each other's freedom.

and you're going to have to deal with it." This felt very unfair to me. I took this as confirmation that she was indeed jealous of me for some reason— but the reason was still a mystery to me.

Eventually, Lisa retired, but her attitude toward me stayed on in my records, causing other managers to overlook me for salary increases as well. Finally, about two years after Lisa retired, Bill was fired and I got his job. That showed me how good a job I had actually done. The new management finally recognized it.

I stayed at that job for twenty-two years, learning many spiritual lessons, doing the best I could. I learned how to stay neutral and keep my attention focused on the positive.

Although it took many years, the situation healed itself by the grace of God. At the time, I didn't remember any past lives related to it. But when I was later exploring the reasons behind the mysteries of that former job, I realized this:

I had been a warrior in a past life, and Lisa was the commander. She treated me then the way she treated me as manager in this life. She wanted to keep me down, not letting me shine and do my best. She was jealous of me in that life because I knew the answers and strategy that escaped her. She was unsure of herself and what to do next. I opened my mouth once too often, giving answers that turned out to be right. She felt guilty that people were dying because of her ineptness but put up a strong front to hide those feelings. There was no confidence behind that wall, however, which is why she didn't like me.

> Although it took many years, the situation healed itself by the grace of God.

How had I created that situation?

In a life before that one, I was a cruel mother to my children. Lisa had been my daughter then. I put her down and called her names. My mother back then had raised me in the same way, so it was all I knew. Bill (my boss in that former job and close friend in this life) was my son, and I favored him. That's why Lisa was so jealous. It explained her anger and lack of caring for Bill too.

DISCOVER THE POWER OF HIGHER LOVE

Love can also be a charitable feeling of goodwill toward others. This is actually a higher form of love. Letting others be comes from practicing this higher love.

Jennifer was able to take on a challenging work relationship using this form of higher love. Her situation involved more than one person, so it was especially difficult. Having learned a unique view of life helped Jennifer handle her situation with grace and courage.

When I'm in the presence of another person with whom I have an issue, I'm often aware it hasn't come from this life. Then I get into what I call the neutral zone, observing the whole interaction from an observer's view. I don't need to put my energy into it, because that would create more conflict. This helps me all day long, every day. It helps me remember that I'm more than just the physical body.

One of two sisters for whom I worked had offered me the job at the very first interview. We

Love can also be a charitable feeling of goodwill toward others. This is actually a higher form of love. Letting others be comes from practicing this higher love.

had a strong connection with each other. This happened with the other sister too. But as time went on, conflicts developed between the two sisters and me. It became so intense, at times I even saw hatred in their eyes. When difficult situations arose, they always thought I was doing something against them. I was so distraught, because I loved them as Soul. It was very painful to me that they thought I had unkind intentions.

I began to realize these misunderstandings were past-life issues. I had to really focus on staying neutral. Maintaining my sense of balance took a lot of practice, spiritual exercises, and help from my inner spiritual guide, the Mahanta.

Eventually the issues with these two sisters did get worked through. The one who hired me got laid off. Even her position was eliminated! I knew then that the past-life's issues had been completed with her and all the others.

Jennifer discovered something very helpful in working out this past-life karma. You don't always have to know exactly what happened in your former incarnation. You may not even want to know! Also, it helps to keep emotions neutral, for your own balance.

Higher, divine love is unconditional. It takes a strong desire to live from a place of pure love while dealing with this physical world. One secret is singing HU every day. It can help you get to and stay in a higher viewpoint.

Would you like to try an exercise that may help

Higher, divine love is unconditional. It takes a strong desire to live from a place of pure love while dealing with this physical world. One secret is singing HU every day.

you stay more neutral, helping heal old karma?

Try the following exercise to see how Soul works inwardly even when we are asleep or unaware.

Exploration Exercise: Meeting of Souls

When you find yourself in conflict with anyone in your life, whether it is related to work, family, or friends, try this technique. You can actually ask to work out the problem inwardly. You may end up meeting the other person in your dreams or another time when you may or may not be aware of what is taking place. Here's how:

1. In a quiet time or just before sleep, ask the Mahanta, or your inner spiritual guide, to help you work out the issue with your friend, family member, or coworker inwardly. Sing HU to become more neutral.

2. Inwardly ask or write down any questions you may have about the difficult situation with this person.

3. Listen for any message from the Mahanta, your inner guide, or God. Watch your dreams, and make note of them for a few days to see if there are any clues. You may find the situation resolves itself—just from your intent to work it out with divine love and neutrality.

Watch your dreams, and make note of them for a few days to see if there are any clues. You may find the situation resolves itself—just from your intent to work it out with divine love and neutrality.

PLEASANT LIFETIMES HELP US REST AND HEAL OLD WOUNDS

Have you ever wondered about someone you met only briefly but with whom you felt a strong attraction or connection?

Lifetimes of experiencing birth and death, fear and courage, and all the other challenges of life can forge lasting bonds between Souls.

Ryan doesn't have to wonder what lifetime forged the instant friendship he recently experienced, because he knows. Here's his story:

Lifetimes of experiencing birth and death, fear and courage, and all the other challenges of life can forge lasting bonds between Souls.

was sitting on an airplane next to a four-year-old, Alison. Very gracefully, her mother asked me if it was OK for her daughter to talk to me. As soon as I said yes, Alison began talking to me, and our conversation continued the entire four-hour flight! We spoke to each other as equals, not child to adult or adult to child. We were in this wonderful world together, as if we'd been friends forever.

Behind us there was a younger child of about two, who kept kicking the back of my seat. Alison said, very maturely, "Oh, these kids just don't know how to act." I knew then and there she was more than a child.

When I left the plane, I realized that this final four-hour segment of a difficult vacation had been the most enjoyable and special part! I felt sad having to leave Alison. It was very hard for me to say good-bye, and I could tell it was hard for her too. I wondered why. When I looked at a possible past-life connection, I got my answer.

I began to see water and trees. I had the feeling Alison and I were pioneers and very good friends, helping each other survive. She was a man in that life, and so was I. We would hunt and forage for food together, living off the land. We protected each other from attacking Indians and wild animals. There were times we had to keep each other from being swept away by strong rapids in the nearby river.

I felt healed from my not-so-great vacation because an old friend was there to give me love. That simple, brief moment in time spoke an eternity to me in terms of love.

The pleasant lifetimes can help us handle difficulties in this life. When we have formed a bond of love or friendship in the past, it often serves as a soothing ointment to quell the hurts of life. William experienced being this kind of friend:

> When we have formed a bond of love or friendship in the past, it often serves as a soothing ointment to quell the hurts of life.

I attended a conference where I met a man who seemed very familiar to me. We had similar understandings about life and decided to get together for dinner. From then on we became good friends, keeping in touch regularly. We even took a vacation together with his son. We all got along very well. This seemed unusual to me, since we had known each other only briefly.

I discovered we had been married to each other in a past life. Even though we are both heterosexual males this lifetime, he was my loving wife in our past life.

The friendship we share has been wonderfully peaceful. We have undoubtedly worked out any karma we had in other lives.

Now my friend calls me when he has relationship problems. I listen and try to be a good friend. He says, "It's so nice to talk with someone I get along so well with! It reminds me that good relationships are possible."

I'm glad I could be a source of healing for a very old friend from the past.

We've all worked hard to get to where we are today. Not every relationship has karma to work out. As William and his friend found out, some relationships can just be a special gift.

IT'S GREAT TO ENJOY WHAT WE HAVE EARNED FROM PAST-LIFE EFFORTS

Even when there's karma to work out in relationships, our lifetimes of learning can support us in that work. So many of our past-life lessons become wonderful tools to apply to any relationship, even with roommates!

Bonnie discovered she had more resources than she knew:

*A*s a roommate, I had always been the neat and clean one. My housemates had to live up to my standards of perfection. I thought I was the most picky housekeeper until I met Gloria. I couldn't believe how neat she was. I had no idea that much neatness even existed! Every single corner and crevice always had to be clean.

Though I liked and respected Gloria, this really bugged me. Now I knew how my former roommates had felt about *me*!

I know life is teaching me spiritual lessons

> So many of our past-life lessons become wonderful tools to apply to any relationship, even with roommates!

all the time, so I looked within to find the pearl of wisdom. Asking the Mahanta, my spiritual teacher and inner guide, what the connection was, I got my answer.

The image of dark and light came to me. Gloria and I were both in positions of power in a previous life as high priests. However, she was working to bring more light into the world, and I was simply looking for power. The image of darkness I saw was the past-life me, and the light was her.

In our previous life together, Gloria's purity had irked me, and that carried into this life. Even though our spiritual purposes were more aligned in this life, our housekeeping wasn't. So I had to face more spiritual tests.

How would I handle the picky details of our living situation.

The answer was patience. My inner guidance said, "Let it rest." So I did, and we are still good friends, even though we are no longer roommates. I found more patience than I knew I had, so it allowed our roommate relationship to evolve into friendship.

I feel like I am a more flexible person now, more spiritually aware.

> We can all develop insights from our past lives that can help us in this one. How we use those tools is up to us.

Like Bonnie, we can all develop insights from our past lives that can help us in this one. How we use those tools is up to us.

It often takes a certain level of self-discipline or courage. And sometimes we are rewarded for our efforts in surprising ways, like receiving an unexpected physical healing.

In the next chapter you will find tools to explore past lives for possible causes of health issues in this life.

6

Past Lives, Present Health

*To properly walk the spiritual path, you
have to be strong enough to carry your own
burdens. At some point you gain the wisdom to
take on fewer spiritual burdens. Soon you find
that life moves along rather nicely. Not always
easily, but nicely. When a problem does come
up, you recognize it for what it is.*

— Harold Klemp, *The Drumbeat of Time,*
Mahanta Transcripts, Book 10[1]

---

*H*ealth issues can be challenging, even with
the wonderful new healing methods available. From traditional medicine to natural means, we
have a profusion of choices. But I know some people
who have tried nearly everything they can find to
resolve a nagging health problem. With no results.

Perhaps you're one of these people. You've been to
doctors, changed your eating and exercise habits, got
more sleep, and tried positive thinking. If nothing has
worked for you, try exploring your past lives. I've found
that it can loosen otherwise immovable health issues.

Your health challenge may not instantly go away.
You may still have some karma to work out. But at

If nothing has
worked for you,
try exploring
your past lives.
I've found that
it can loosen
otherwise
immovable
health issues.

least you'll gain an understanding of the cause, like Gerard in the story below.

I've always had problems with my teeth; it's caused me great pain at times. Porous teeth from birth required metal caps at a very young age, then came cavities, root canals, and finally false teeth.

I discovered I was a torturer in a past life, and yes, my specialty was teeth.

My porous teeth in this life gave me a gift; a reminder of an important lesson from the past: that love is greater than power.

> Even the physical body holds a treasure trove of spiritual lessons.

Even the physical body holds a treasure trove of spiritual lessons. We may not think of them as treasures when we're in pain. But to see all life as a gift can get us through the most distressing, uncomfortable circumstances. I have often felt the most love surrounding me when I have been in the worst pain. When I accepted that love, God's love, it healed me.

As Harold Klemp says, "The power of love is always stronger than the fear of karma."[2]

IT TAKES COURAGE TO LOOK AT HOW WE'VE CAUSED OUR OWN PAIN

Jill had great strength and courage in dealing with a very uncomfortable, painful, and frustrating condition.

I had a terrible rash most of my life. As a young child, I scratched my arms and legs until they bled.

Growing up, I got very tired of this rash and

went to a nontraditional doctor who came highly recommended. This doctor told me my rash was not caused by a physical condition but was psychological. He asked me if I would like to do a guided visualization to look at what the cause might be. I was fully awake and aware. He simply helped me relax and allow myself to access any subconscious images. This is the experience I had:

I was aware of being a prostitute in a past life. This did not shock me as I visualized it, because it was just the way it was. I had a problem in that life relating to men in a non-sexual way. I developed a sexually transmitted disease and died from it.

I was aware of still feeling guilty about that former life on a subconscious level. Then I realized I felt as though I actually deserved the rash, because of this guilt from the past.

I had to let go of the guilt. This was not really me, but an experience in another life.

Once I let it go, the rash went away. This didn't happen instantly, but over time it completely healed.

It's exciting to learn that problems in this life have deeper spiritual roots. Changes usually take place over time, as we gain greater and greater understanding of the root cause.

Not all people are as fortunate as Jill. Some afflictions may be permanent in this lifetime due to the nature of the illness. This is based upon life karma where everything is set up before birth for a lifetime or partial lifetime condition, in order to work out a heavy load of karma in this life.

Shawna has been physically challenged for over

Some afflictions may be permanent in this lifetime due to the nature of the illness.

half her life with paralysis. She was generous enough to share her story.

*W*hen I was eleven years old, my house burned down with my parents still in it. My two sisters and I were out of town, so we were safe. But we were now homeless, without our parents.

My life was never the same. Sometimes I wondered why I had survived. Little did I know it was so I could work out even more karma from the past.

In my first year of college, about thirty years ago, I let a friend drive my car, and we had a head-on collision. Because we were in the country, it took a long time for me to get treated. The lack of circulation traumatized my spine and put me in a wheelchair. I felt so lost and alone, more than ever before. I felt like I was in a big, empty place, not knowing what or who to hold on to or where to go. I had to accept that the only resource I had was myself.

I had always liked to ask myself, What am I learning from this? But this time I could not figure out the answer. The situation was too new.

Before being in a wheelchair, I was insecure sometimes, but I knew myself. I knew I would muddle through no matter what happened. But now that I was in the chair, I thought, *What can I do now?*

I used to do my thinking by walking. I would talk to my guardian angels or whoever was there (now I know it was the Mahanta, my inner spiritual guide) and figure things out that way. Now I couldn't even walk! So for some reason, I felt as if I couldn't think or even feel connected

I used to do my thinking by walking. I would talk to my guardian angels or whoever was there (now I know it was the Mahanta, my inner spiritual guide) and figure things out that way.

to my inner guidance.

It was awful to feel so alone. And the feeling wouldn't lift.

Finally I began to explore my past lives to see how they might connect to this experience and help me understand the spiritual lesson in this lifetime of karma. I remembered three lives that helped me understand it all.

In the first lifetime, I was friends with a man who was some kind of public protector, like a policeman. I was female and had a strong inner connection to this man. I wanted something more than just a friendship, but that was all it ever was. I was also attracted to him because he was an authority figure and I had a strong need for approval and acceptance. My need for acceptance came from the fact that when I was about eleven years old, my parents had gone away and never come back. Somehow, in that culture, it was the custom to leave a grown child, yet I was not ready.

In the next lifetime, I was on a Viking ship as a young boy, helping wherever I could and not being treated very well. Again, I felt very much alone. I had been born to an unwed mother who was unable to take care of me. She knew some-one on the ship who could take me and raise me to be a deckhand. I worked hard from an early age but was always alone, always lonely.

The third lifetime I recalled was one that showed me the seed cause for both of the other lifetimes to occur—as well as this present life of sadness and loneliness.

I was a very cruel man in a western town during the pioneer days. I controlled everyone and everything. I would walk into stores and

The third lifetime I recalled was one that showed me the seed cause for both of the other lifetimes to occur—as well as this present life of sadness and loneliness.

take what I wanted then ride away.

If anyone tried to stop me, I would kill them with my bare hands, breaking their neck. Or at the very least, I would break an arm. The son of a lumberjack, I was extremely strong. My father was very strong as well, and perhaps didn't know his own strength because he would beat me until I was black and blue or bleeding—otherwise, he didn't consider it enough punishment for whatever the minor infraction.

When I looked at that life from the Soul viewpoint, I realized my father had been beaten by his father as well. They were both trying to teach right from wrong. I took it to the extreme. I thought I had a right to everything I wanted and thought it wrong for anyone to stop me. Someone finally did stop me with a knife, and that was the end of my life of tyranny.

Because I had left many families without a father in that life, I had to endure loneliness and physical disabilities in this life, as a karmic lesson.

Now I could see the answer to my question thirty years before, What am I supposed to learn from this? It was to learn the power of love. Love conquers all. I realized that when love isn't there, problems arise.

I notice now that when I look at everything with a forgiving love, or even when I think of the word *love*, it melts the bad things away.

Love is calming and can soften even anger—inasmuch as I am willing to accept love.

> Love is calming and can soften even anger—inasmuch as I am willing to accept love.

Like any emotion, guilt will come up and be experienced at times. Letting it go is important. Knowing we're simply learning as we go may help.

KNOW YOU'RE LEARNING SOMETHING, EVEN WHEN YOU THINK YOU'RE NOT

When we're having any kind of painful experience, it can teach us something in a very quiet way. Perhaps we don't understand exactly what we're learning until we look back. Sometimes we must look back further than we think. Trevor had no idea how far back he'd have to look to find the answer to a devastating dysfunction:

> I was raised in this life as a very strict Catholic. I had a lot of guilt. I noticed a problem with sexual thoughts. I started compulsively washing my hands, because I felt so guilty. In addition, I repressed all my sexual energy.
>
> As I grew older and began to date, I started having a relationship with a girl. There was some sexual karma and guilt issues about making love. The guilt turned into a constant fear and anxiety, causing me unbearable physical pain. I had to end the relationship. The anxiety calmed down immediately.
>
> I didn't understand what was going on. I really wanted love in my life, so I met someone else and started a new relationship. I developed the same symptoms. But I always had an excuse—it was the person I was dating, not me!
>
> Time after time, the pattern repeated itself. My last serious girlfriend was Becky. I fell head over heals in love with her. We had a wonderful, uplifting love. I thought for sure I would marry her. The farther I fell in love with her, the more anxiety I experienced, just like with the others.

When we're having any kind of painful experience, it can teach us something in a very quiet way. Perhaps we don't understand exactly what we're learning until we look back.

At this point in my life, I found my spiritual connection. I began asking God to help me to grow spiritually. I wanted to be as spiritual as I could, as fast as I could!

This desire to grow too fast brought up old junk from the subconscious level. I was pulled into a nightmare where I began to have horrible anxiety twenty-four hours a day and a pain in my stomach that I had never experienced before. It drove me to my knees.

Ten being the worst imaginable level of anxiety, I was at level eight or nine. I had to use all my willpower just to get out of bed and go to work. I dreaded weekends, because I had to be with myself. I would sit by the riverbank and cry.

I finally went to a doctor and had a lower gastrointestinal exploration done. They could not find any physical problem. The stomach pain continued for a couple of years.

Then I decided to attend a spiritual retreat. I asked God to find a way to show me, at the retreat, what was going on with this pain. I asked to see some past lives, if they were related to the pain.

The day before the retreat I had a dream that showed me I would be getting some kind of answer to my problem.

While I was at the retreat, I recalled nine different past lives that tied in to this pain in my abdomen. I had been injured or killed by some blow or cut to my stomach area.

The main past life occurred in the Middle Ages; I lived in a feudal society in England. I had gotten into a lot of trouble because I marched to my own drummer; I was a free spirit and a free-

> I asked God to find a way to show me, at the retreat, what was going on with this pain. I asked to see some past lives, if they were related to the pain.

thinker. I had found a scroll that contained something about the sexual tantric yoga techniques. I experimented with a woman and was caught. I was put to death, impaled on a huge stick. The woman in that life is Becky in this life.

After these past-life recalls I thought the anxiety problem might go away. I started a new relationship with hope but the same patterns surfaced. The stomach pain was so bad, I stayed in bed for eighteen hours. I told my new girlfriend we had to stop our sexual relationship. I eventually broke up with her.

On top of the pain and anxiety, I started getting mentally muddled. This affected my work. I was a computer programmer, a total intellectual. But the fuzzy-headed feeling got worse, and the anxiety got worse.

Life was definitely trying to send me a message, but what was it?

Finally, someone asked me, "What caused those nine lifetimes of being attacked? You're never just a victim, you know."

That made me sit up and take notice. That's what I was missing! I'd forgotten that I might have attacked someone too. Indeed I had!

Right away I got three different past-life images.

In one lifetime I had chopped off someone's head for sleeping with my wife. I had never forgiven her.

In another life I had abused someone sexually.

In a third lifetime, I was a physically abusive parent.

It was time to forgive those who had hurt me and myself for being the one who had hurt others.

Life was definitely trying to send me a message, but what was it? Finally, someone asked me, "What caused those nine lifetimes of being attacked? You're never just a victim, you know."

Having the understanding of what I had done to cause my pain and guilt has been the key: it has finally helped me move ahead. Over time, the pain and anxiety have diminished and finally disappeared. The greatest miracle is I am getting married soon!

Even small aches and pains that persist are important to observe. They may be trying to tell us that there is a spiritual lesson we can learn more easily, so we don't have to go through a larger experience with more suffering.

Nicole's lesson from a past life came through her neck. She resolved most of the pain in realizing and understanding a past-life memory.

> Even small aches and pains that persist are important to observe. They may be trying to tell us that there is a spiritual lesson we can learn more easily, so we don't have to go through a larger experience with more suffering.

I wondered why I had a problem with chronic neck pain. It had always been the weakest area of my body. I often got a stiff, sore neck or sore throat. The answer came in a dream.

In the dream I was living in the south as an African-American during post-slavery times. I was hung, which was fairly common in that era for a black man who did anything to cross the lines set up by white men. However, the hanging was very long and painful because of the way it was done. I suffered quite a bit before I died, and I certainly did not forgive my executioners.

I was an angry and outspoken young man in that life. I readily expressed my feelings in public about how people of my race were being treated. My temper got the best of me. I was unable to relax and let go, accept the way things were in that imperfect society. Since I was much more vocal about these affairs than I safely could be,

I was punished severely and set up as an example for anyone who would dare to be like me.

In realizing the cause of my neck pain, I learned how important it is to be aware of what you can and cannot do with what you've chosen in each life. If I had controlled my emotions better, I may have lived much longer and perhaps even made a difference in a safer, quieter way. I also learned that forgiveness has its benefits. Once I was able to forgive my killers, I was free. My neck has improved tremendously since then!

Janette had a different kind of "pain in the neck." Her throat is much better now thanks to the help and understanding she got from two past-life recalls.

I frequently got sore throats that would turn into other illnesses. These bouts would last weeks at a time! My throat would feel constricted. Even though my lifestyle included healthy food and exercise balanced with rest, and my spiritual life was rich with spiritual exercises and trusting my inner guide, the Mahanta. I was frustrated with this chronic problem. What else could I do?

I knew I had to look to past lives for the answer.

I was talking to a friend about it, telling her how I often felt like I was being strangled. How I would become depressed and down on myself, even having suicidal thoughts. This was not my real self, and I knew it.

I explored the possibilities in this conversation with my trusted friend and discovered I actually had been strangled—in a former life.

> In realizing the cause of my neck pain, I learned how important it is to be aware of what you can and cannot do with what you've chosen in each life.

My husband in that life had been an alcoholic and was very abusive. In a drunken rage, he ended up killing me.

I wondered how I had earned the karma of that lifetime. I came up with an answer that was devastating. Many lifetimes before, I had killed a spiritual teacher. This was during a time when Christianity was the prominent religion. My family and friends were fighting anything that wasn't in alignment with our beliefs. I was a headstrong young man and decided I would step forward to eliminate the evil intruder.

In the moment I killed him, I saw only pure love and acceptance in his eyes. I immediately thought, *Oh, God, I've made a terrible mistake.* I died with shame. That shame carried into many lifetimes. I have now finally been able to let it go.

I've had a healthy throat for two years now because I finally forgave myself and let go of the past.

ASK FOR HELP FROM GOD WHEN YOU NEED IT

Asking for help from the Holy Spirit is what brought health back to Jacqueline's lungs and joy back into her life.

> Asking for help from the Holy Spirit is what brought health back to Jacqueline's lungs and joy back into her life.

I've had lung problems for about seven years, usually in the form of bronchitis. One summer I contracted pneumonia, losing quite a bit of time at work. I had always been healthy, and this was really upsetting to me. I decided I was going to get to the bottom of this.

Knowing past-life karma might hold a clue,

I asked the Holy Spirit for an answer and became aware of the following past life.

It was around A.D. 600. I was a knight on a campaign in Wales. I was very haughty and superficial; my personality was not endearing! I remember a foggy day at twilight when I was supposed to be watching for the enemy. However, the enemy found me first. A lowly foot soldier attacked me from behind and speared me in the ribs, right through the lungs. He literally pulled me off my high horse.

Somehow I survived the attack, but I was very disgruntled. *How dare a mere peasant boy find and attack me when I was on watch?* I thought.

For the rest of my life I was in pain whenever it was damp, and of course, it was damp nearly all the time in Wales. Rather than being humble and grateful for my life, I was never happy. I was rich and had servants to wait on me constantly, but I whined and complained about everything. If I was in pain, everyone else must suffer as well.

Once I remembered that past life, I immediately made the connection in this life. I've had a tendency to be discontent and easily disgruntled, especially as a child. Having carried my miserable black knight attitude into this life, I couldn't be content and grateful for this life, until I let go of that lifetime and that experience.

I did begin to let go of my past unhappiness and grief. Now the joy is seeping in, and there is more room for love and gratitude. I'm also grateful for a healthy body, and there has been a marked improvement in my lungs. I have no physical deformities in this life, and I am

Once I remembered that past life, I immediately made the connection in this life.

learning to be thankful for that too.

I've come to realize something remarkable from that experience. This is a golden lifetime. The choices we are making right now are creating events in our future lives, wherever they may be, even in the heavenly worlds. I'm starting to choose life instead of life choosing me. I realize I'm free to break karmic patterns with the help of the Mahanta, my inner guide.

> This is a golden lifetime. The choices we are making right now are creating events in our future lives, wherever they may be, even in the heavenly worlds.

This Is a Golden Lifetime of Choice

Jaqueline's discovery of her right of choice gave her more freedom than she had ever imagined possible. You have that same right of choice. Continue to ask for help in knowing what your choices are. There are many ways to get this help, including in your dreams.

Laura received help in her dreams when she wondered why she was having kidney problems.

The problems with my kidneys were always accompanied by pain in the kidney area. One night, I had a dream that someone was beating me, particularly around the kidney area of my back. I yelled at the man to get away from me and never return. I woke up very angry, knowing immediately who had been beating me.

It was Henry, an abusive husband from a past life in London.

We had lived in a dirty, sooty neighborhood in the 1880s. Life was not easy for Henry. Finally, he beat me so hard that he destroyed my kidneys. I had writhed in pain for three days until I finally died of kidney failure.

Then I looked back on a visit to England in this life when I was sixteen years old. I had hated it, especially London. There was a sense of malice for me there, particularly in one section of the city. It seemed nice enough in present times, but there was a sensation that I had died there. I definitely did not want to be anywhere near that neighborhood.

From that life, I was learning to set boundaries, to not tolerate being a victim, even if I loved someone. I discovered I don't have to let anybody in, just because I know them, even if it's only in my dreams.

Many of us have experienced trauma that has followed us into more than one life. Sherry's asthma is from a past-life trauma. She knew her asthma related to a past life, but not which one. As she contemplated on where this problem may have come from, an image came to her.

*I*t was in the early 1800s somewhere in the western United States. I was riding my horse along a path beneath a rocky area, and I was taken by surprise when a rock slide quickly covered me and my horse. Something fell on my chest. The first thing I felt was total panic. It was hard to let go of life. I was not resigned to dying and was really ticked off about it!

Sherry was actually laughing at this point in the interview, because since that wild lifetime she's learned that death is an illusion. It seems to be so final, yet it's simply a doorway to another life of greater learning for Soul.

I was learning to set boundaries, to not tolerate being a victim, even if I loved someone.

Divine Guidance Can Help Us Find More Joy in This Life

When we find spiritual guidance and direction from God, an understanding may come about to show us why we have difficulties and help us see a higher purpose.

"Insights into the spiritual reason for happenings in everyday life are often more revealing of the ways that the Holy Spirit uses to lift each of us to be better spiritual creatures,"[3] writes Harold Klemp. When we find spiritual guidance and direction from God, an understanding may come about to show us why we have difficulties and help us see a higher purpose.

Joanna decided she would focus on divine guidance in her own life to help her daughter get through a very difficult health problem. She was astonished to discover a healing for herself, as well as for her daughter!

Joanna's daughter Emmy had attention deficit disorder. Here's what happened that triggered a past-life recall, strengthening Joanna's emotions and helping Emmy.

Emmy was a real handful, even on ADD medication. We tried everything. We went to five different doctors without getting results. We couldn't keep Emmy on medication because of a rebound effect. It was a nightmare!

I really wanted to help my daughter but didn't know what else to do. Finally, after giving up on everything else, I wrote a letter to God asking for help. Then something changed.

I became aware that I too had something to learn from my daughter's illness. When she acted out, stomping her foot and saying no to the smallest request, I began to see the roles she and I were playing.

I knew she had been my mother in a past

life during the 1700s in America. She was very strong, powerful, and domineering. I loved her anyway, and this love helped me know how to handle her in this life. As I explored this further and became more aware of my daughter's role in my own spiritual unfoldment, I saw what to do.

I needed to learn to stand up for myself and not let her control me, while not crushing her independent spirit.

She became a wonderful mirror for me. Knowing she was reflecting qualities I needed to work out within myself, I realized she was a blessing. She was helping me strengthen my weak spots!

Now she is grown up, working at a good job, even going back to school to begin a professional career! She did make it, contrary to the limited expectations of others. I have made it too. I have learned to stand up for myself, an important lesson.

Jaqueline became acutely aware, by studying a previous life, of the cause for repeated injuries when she was a child.

For a period of about three to five years I was continually hurting my knees, especially the right one. Falling often, I would usually limp home with big gashes and cuts in my knees.

I have always loved animals, yet I had a definite dislike for horses. The mystery of my constant knee injuries and my dislike for horses cleared up when I recalled a past life.

This recall was triggered by the comments of a friend who is a dancer. She asked me if I

> I needed to learn to stand up for myself and not let her control me, while not crushing her independent spirit.
> She became a wonderful mirror for me. Knowing she was reflecting qualities I needed to work out within myself, I realized she was a blessing.

was a dancer. She said I had the carriage and bearing of a trained dancer.

That's when I realized that in a former life, I was trained from a very early age to be a prima ballerina. That goal was everything to me. I was very disciplined to the point of austerity and self-denial. My friendships suffered and eventually disappeared due to my complete focus. I was proud of my self-discipline and disdainful of others who were less focused. I became very lonely, but I considered that an acceptable sacrifice for my art.

I did reach my goal of becoming a successful dancer, earning worldwide acclaim. But just as I was rising to stardom, I sustained a crushing blow to my career. A horse I was riding tripped, and we fell.

My knees were both broken in the accident. This was the end of my dancing career, the only life I knew. Somehow, though, I could never manage to get off my high horse.

Looking at the experiences in my ballerina lifetime taught me that love and humility are more important than willpower or self-denial. Self-discipline must be balanced with love and friendship. The only healing for me in that life would have been to open my heart, so now, in this life, I do.

Acting with love every day takes rare courage, humility, and self-discipline.

OPENING THE HEART IS THE ULTIMATE HEALING TECHNIQUE

Acting with love every day takes rare courage, humility, and self-discipline. But it also takes an open heart. How can we keep our hearts open?

Some situations are gifts of love because both people's hearts are open.

Two hearts were open in the case of Rose and her doctor. The healing that took place was speedy and beyond normal expectations. Rose tells her story:

I was new to the city and went out running in a state park with a friend. My leg suddenly flew out from under me, and I fell in a heap. The pain was intense, so I told her to call 911.

Two ambulances arrived, and one took me to the hospital in a nearby town that used to be in Native American territory. The doctor was wonderful and very kind. He repaired my broken femur perfectly, putting a pin in it.

By the time it healed, my leg was stronger than it had ever been! It occurred to me later that I broke the leg because I was paying back some karmic debt, but what was it?

I wondered why I broke the leg and how I deserved to be so lucky in the healing process. Being a strong believer in past lives, I explored the possibility using my intuition and going with the images that sprung to mind. I came up with this:

Two Native American boys were playing together. I was one of them. I lived in the same area I now live, but centuries before. Somehow I hurt the other boy in a way that seemed like playing but was a dangerous move. I felt very badly about hurting his leg, but he recovered.

I realized eventually that the kind doctor who healed me was the friend I had hurt in that life. He was forgiving me and completing the cycle of healing. His love for me brought us together.

My heart has opened so much more from this powerful experience of love and forgiveness!

My heart has opened so much more from this powerful experience of love and forgiveness!

Lisa was open to exploring past lives as well. She wanted to get answers to hard questions about her eating disorder.

Lisa had lived with this terrible challenge most of her life. In a double bind, she was afraid of food and afraid she wouldn't get enough food. This paradox plagued her until she discovered reincarnation and its possible explanation for her dilemma.

Here's Lisa's story:

When I was little, I used to be really focused on food. I needed to be sure it was always available. When I spent the night at a friend's house, if they didn't eat breakfast, I would call my mom, crying because I was hungry.

I ate a lot of food at mealtimes. I could eat more than anybody in my family, and I was the youngest! I always took food with me wherever I went. My mom knew how scared I was of starving, so she would pack a grocery bag full of food for me!

As I grew older and more conscious of my figure, I developed an eating disorder. I'd binge and starve, binge and starve.

Then I had three dreams showing me I'd lived through the Holocaust. In the first dream, I was very young and pretty and had a tempting offer, a way out. I could have accepted a proposal to live with a German officer who would say I wasn't Jewish. But I refused to do that. So, with my brother, I was taken to a concentration camp, where food was very scarce. Many people starved to death.

In another dream, my head was being shaved. I had long beautiful hair, and it hurt me so much to see it all shaved off. I knew I was in a concentration camp. (In my present life I have always worn my hair long.)

In the third dream, all my possessions were taken away. I saw the room where the jewels, clothing, and gold fillings were placed. This was also in a concentration camp. Then we were shot.

I knew from these dreams I had lived during the Holocaust where meals—if you got a meal—consisted of watery soup and, if you were very lucky, a small crust of stale bread. This helped me make the connection between why I worried about food, why I hoarded food, and always made sure I had enough. Once I was aware of the reason for my obsession with food, it healed over time.

Understanding that scarcity is no longer a concern in my life, since my karma is finished with that lifetime, I trust the Holy Spirit to provide what I need. I now have a balanced, healthy attitude about food and have even started a career teaching health and nutrition classes.

Sometimes just awareness of a past life will help bring about a healing. It may take awhile, but healing will usually come over time as you let go of the past with the recognition that it *is* past, knowing you've learned the lessons you needed to learn.

Unexplained chronic disorders may be trying to remind us to forgive the past to help us heal now.

How can you get a spiritual healing of a present disorder or injury that may be rooted in a past-life issue?

We can do this through love, greater awareness, and forgiveness. These spiritual qualities bring us

> Sometimes just awareness of a past life will help bring about a healing.

closer to God. Try this next exercise as a means to loving yourself.

Exploration Exercise:

Healing with Light and Sound

1. Find a quiet, pleasant place to sit or lay down with your eyes closed.

2. Look inside at where you hurt the most or feel the most discomfort in your body.

3. Imagine a blue light moving into that area. Blue light is very healing to the emotions. Think of the most beautiful sound or music you can imagine. If you don't hear any, simply sing the word *HU* to yourself. Fill the area with both the blue light and this healing sound.

Even if healing isn't immediate, you may receive a greater understanding of the past-life connection and what you need to learn from your health issue.

Enjoy the simplicity of this healing exercise every day, for as long as it takes to bring about some relief. Even if healing isn't immediate, you may receive a greater understanding of the past-life connection and what you need to learn from your health issue.

In the next chapter, spiritual progress through careers and finances is illustrated through some unique past-life stories.

7

Careers Under Past-Life Management

Soul is always in charge of Its own destiny.
This is why I'm trying to bring out the information that you are Soul. It lifts you from the material to the spiritual consciousness. Then it's just a matter of sticking with it and allowing this consciousness to grow in you—that you are Soul and you can do something about your life.

— Harold Klemp, *What Is Spiritual Freedom?*
Mahanta Transcripts, Book 11[1]

Soul is always in charge of Its own destiny.

---

*E*ver wonder why the same problems surface at different jobs, over and over again?

Or why some people are drawn to certain careers and love them?

Or why others seem to be held back from a higher level of income?

I've asked these questions myself, when I felt like I was hitting a financial wall and couldn't break through. I eventually discovered I had lived past lives as a terrifying tax collector and as a resident of debtor's prison. I began to see the effects of other lifetimes that held me back in my job and finances in this one.

Repeated career or financial issues may stem from past-life distress. Even if financial limits have been placed on you in your present life, you may have imported even more intense patterns from a previous life. Sometimes this is necessary to finish the lesson. But with a little effort, Soul can realize the spiritual lesson and harvest the spiritual fruits.

The following group of people put some effort into their past-life exploration to better understand their careers and finances. Each came up with spiritual gold.

Ellen had to go to California to find her spiritual gold, long after the original gold rush.

Within three months of marrying, Ellen and her new husband moved to California from their beautiful mountain home in Montana. She did not want to go, but this move was her husband's major dream. Ellen expressed her distress about this experience:

We visited California before moving, and I knew I didn't want to live there. I wasn't comfortable there. However, my husband needed to live there for a job he really wanted to take. Since there was no apparent outer reason for my discomfort, I agreed to go. As soon as we crested the ridge of mountains on our drive to California, I got this huge feeling of dread.

Life was very difficult from the start. It was too expensive—from the rent on our apartment to food. Everything was uncomfortable to me. Even the plants everyone loved in California were unappealing. During our years there I always felt unsettled. Gradually I became aware of a strong sense of a past life during the California gold rush. Then I remembered the details of that previous existence.

Leaving family and friends behind, I had joined the others on the California trail. We all had the impossible dream of striking gold in that lifetime, and I ended up working a menial job just to survive.

In this lifetime, I had always been able to survive on my art and live off the land out in the country, which I loved doing. Going back to California set up a very tight financial structure for me. Without a college degree, I had to accept menial jobs! My last lifetime in California was duplicating itself.

I learned adaptation to survive. I became creative in ways I would have never pushed myself into before. I was forced to grow as an artist. Developing creative work that brought a higher income also made me evolve professionally, as well as spiritually. I was forced to find my gold by digging deeper within myself! In this life, I discovered, my spiritual growth is the real gold.

When we can move beyond our self-imposed prison, as Ellen did in the previous story, we expand our awareness of who we really are—an unlimited spiritual being we call Soul.

EXPANDING OUR LIMITS EXPANDS OUR AWARENESS

One kind of spiritual strength is flexibility, as Ellen so beautifully illustrated. Being flexible allows us to stretch ourselves, to see beyond our present

When we can move beyond our self-imposed prison, we expand our awareness of who we really are—an unlimited spiritual being we call Soul.

circumstances. This helps us hop over today's limits, creating a greater view and awareness of life.

Patrick broke some limits too, while maintaining a career he enjoys.

*T*his lifetime I have always wanted to work in isolation, and I did so for a while as a researcher. Then I decided I wanted to break that pattern, and I became a teacher. Even though I liked teaching, it felt like too much exposure for me. I decided to go into computer programming, which would allow more isolation. I started becoming introverted again.

What is this pattern about? I wondered.

When I explored the past-life possibilities, I discovered I had been a scholar and theologian as a monk. Every day I researched, wrote, and reflected on my findings. I had loved that life of solitude, and I turned more and more inward. It served me well in that life, but it also created a fear of moving outside of solitude.

When I realized it was time to make a change in this life, I began to make efforts to extend myself to others in my work and other activities.

I can see how my upbringing in this life played on and accentuated my past-life fears. My parents encouraged caution and worry. They'd say things like, "Don't extend yourself or exert yourself too much. Be very careful and cautious. Don't take chances; stay home and study." This hampered my self-confidence. It became harder to go out and meet people. It also brought all of the past-life concerns about focus and privacy to the surface, allowing me to work it out in this life.

> When I realized it was time to make a change in this life, I began to make efforts to extend myself to others in my work and other activities.

Now I'm learning to develop more of a social life, more connection. I talk with people on the phone quite a bit for business and volunteer work. Some situations these days require me to network. I can now surrender to the process, because it's necessary to do a good job for my company. I know it's good for me too.

My past life served as a good teacher in several lessons. I gleaned from that life the importance of focus. I learned to eliminate distractions and concentrate on the task at hand. However, I also learned I can get so caught up in this focus I may forget to communicate with other people and reach out to them. A person can get lured too far into themselves. I'm learning to balance that.

Some people may need to experience the pain of a past life in order to heal in their work life today. Claire found this to be the case for her.

*A*fter setting a goal to start my own business, I ran into a brick wall. The obstacle was within *me*. I felt so uncomfortable being my own boss. Strange sensations arose as I began to think about working alone. Somehow, it did not feel OK for me to be successful. I felt like I needed a partner or someone above me, someone I could create success with or for. This was very distressing, as I really wanted the independence to work on my own and earn a good income doing so!

What was going on here?

Why did I feel so dependent on others for my success?

I decided to explore the past to find any lives

Some people may need to experience the pain of a past life in order to heal in their work life today.

that were still holding me back. What I found was much more than I expected.

Every single "career" I remember in a past life was as a slave or concubine. Otherwise, I was somehow subservient, even as a member of a family. I was a slave in Egypt, a concubine somewhere else, a geisha in another life, and a slave in several more. I was not allowed to express what I felt, I couldn't say what I wanted, and I was never in control.

These lifetimes affected the feelings I have about being my own boss. My reluctance to succeed on my own made sense. To act on my own would have been death in those lifetimes.

There were so many lifetimes of this sort of experience, I've had to allow myself time to grieve. In those lifetimes I couldn't express how I felt. Now I can express my feelings and have been doing so ever since! I found there is sometimes a grieving process that cannot be cut short.

As I heal and let go of old emotions, I'm beginning to get closer to who I really am—a positive, happy, and productive Soul.

YOU ARE A SHINING BEING, FREE TO CHOOSE YOUR PATH

Soul is free, naturally, because we have free will. Sometimes our freedom is challenged to make us stronger spiritual beings, stronger in spirit. Yvonne exemplifies someone who is strong in facing past-life challenges to choose her own path in music:

Soul is free, naturally, because we have free will. Sometimes our freedom is challenged to make us stronger spiritual beings, stronger in spirit.

'*ve sung my whole life. As soon as I was old enough to become aware that people were listening to me sing, however, a fear came over me. It changed from childlike singing, singing from the joy of being alive. I became afraid, even sad and melancholy, when I sang. Yet I also felt a longing to sing. I grew up still singing but feeling these new emotions. I even felt a pain in my throat when I sang. I wondered why, but I still sang because I had to.

Just recently the Mahanta showed me the root of the fear. As I was falling asleep and lightly putting my attention on the problem, I got very clear images. I was shown that the fear comes from several past lives.

One of those was a past life in Asia, centuries ago. Live theater was the only form of entertainment. I was a woman who sang about all the emotional pain that society could not accept, like the pain of romantic love. It was too unconventional for the times. I even had unbound hair, which for me represented a state of unconventional freedom. I was singing about freedom too, and they felt I was a threat to women, so while I was onstage my throat was slit.

In another life, I was in France in the fifteenth century. I was a young woman, a well-known singer who played harp and lute. I was called to entertain in the royal court. I remember getting ready for my performance for the king, feeling the coolness and dampness of the air. I knew something bad was going to happen, but there was nothing I could do but follow through with my performance. Afterward, I was captured by order of the king, because he wanted me for himself. I never sang again. I had a vision of being kept in a really dark place. I was told I was one of his subjects and belonged to the

> As I was falling asleep and lightly putting my attention on the problem, I got very clear images. I was shown that the fear comes from several past lives.

king. I stopped singing, I was so stifled. It was the end of my freedom to sing. That king is my father in this lifetime. In this life he is trying to help me with my singing career. He paid for studio time, bought me a guitar, and constantly asks me if I'm singing.

So the fear that followed me into this life is a fear of being captured if people hear me sing. It's the fear of expressing the beauty and freedom of Soul. If I were caught, I'd be like a caged bird, as I was in that previous life.

The third lifetime is where the sadness came from. I was the matriarch of a Scottish clan. Music was as important to us as food, because it was part of our survival. Times were so hard, music was a way of celebrating, savoring that we could sing and dance. There was a lot of turmoil. The English were trying to take over Scotland at that time. The clans had to migrate because food was scarce, and we were hunted down. Music was a way of keeping aware of the joy for life, the hope and courage. Every child was raised knowing all the ballads and songs and stories of the clan. It was my role as the matriarch of the clan to keep that tradition alive.

Because it was such rugged country, we were extremely close. It was the tightest bond you can imagine. I was the main singer of the clan. I taught the ballads to the children and kept our music alive through my voice.

People put all their trust in me. I was also very intuitive and I had a part in knowing what was to come. We all ended up being slaughtered. I felt it was my responsibility, even though it wasn't. To this day I cry when I hear bagpipes.

> Music was a way of keeping aware of the joy for life, the hope and courage.

Because of that life, when I sing now, I feel I am taking on a certain responsibility and there is a fear that responsibility will lead to ruin.

As I'm letting go of these images, my voice is getting stronger. The pain in my throat that I always get when I sing (from having it slit) is going away. The tone of sorrow I always hear in my voice is going away and being replaced by a tone of joy. Now I'm going into the recording studio to forward my career.

In this next story, Mark discovers more about who he really is. He did this by letting go of what others think he should do (from their past-life memories of him). These friends and family members were not aware they knew Mark in a past life; the feelings just came subconsciously. It was a test for Mark to stand up for what he wanted in *this* life, no matter what anyone else said or what talents he'd developed in the past.

It was a test for Mark to stand up for what he wanted in this *life, no matter what anyone else said or what talents he'd developed in the past.*

When I was younger, everyone I knew told me I should go into medicine or some sort of healing arts. They must have seen a talent or ability I had from a past life. I finally remembered that I was some sort of healer in ancient China, as well as a nurse during a war. In the Middle Ages I was a physician. My friends and family obviously were aware of this on some level, though not consciously.

I have always been drawn to healing. At an early age I was reading medical books and journals. At age ten, I perfectly reconstructed an animal skeleton. Eventually I went into premed studies, but that wasn't my love. Finally, I found my love in Chinese medicine.

Later, I realized I had to broaden my perspective of medicine if I was to grow spiritually. The lifetime in China as a healer was a happy one and made me want to stay with Chinese medicine. I had had lifetimes of experience in allopathic medicine as well.

After practicing as an acupuncturist and holistic-health practitioner, I decided I didn't really like being in private practice. Even though I helped the people who came to me, it didn't fulfill me like it should. It just didn't fit me anymore.

What would make me happy? I wondered.

I discovered I enjoyed research. I also liked teaching and training other health practitioners, as well as laypeople. Now I work with all of my talents and continue to research, study, and train at professional seminars in various areas of health.

I also understand that I am here to grow and unfold as a spiritual being. I can always take another step beyond my past-life training. Finding out what makes me happy and learning more about my career doesn't just help my patients and those I teach. It helps me expand my awareness of life.

> Jerome's improved self-esteem was a bonus when spiritual awareness helped him discover past lives affecting his ability to have a fulfilling career.

Jerome's improved self-esteem was a bonus when spiritual awareness helped him discover past lives affecting his ability to have a fulfilling career.

I was in such distress and trauma over not being able to find a career or job where I could be happy or successful. Every time I started something I thought would work well, it failed or I couldn't seem to get to a break-even point. I couldn't even earn enough money to support my family. I finally declared bankruptcy.

As I began to sink lower and lower, some interesting sensations emerged. The first feeling was murky, as if I was drowning in a swamp. I felt so restricted, like I couldn't seem to ever get ahead no matter what I did. Then past-life images began to come to me.

I was a hunchback, or someone like the Elephant Man. Some great physical defect held me back, even though I had clarity of mind. Other people could not accept my appearance long enough to find out what was behind it. That lifetime was very discouraging.

Another life, where I felt like a failure, occurred in the Civil War era. I was seventeen or eighteen years old and ready to leave home, to break out and be free. However, something was holding me back. I wanted so much to go out and fight in the war but I was ill. Finally, I got well enough to leave to fight. But still weak from my illness, I got killed in the war immediately. It was so frustrating to finally be able to get out, yet die so soon before I could be free and help my country be free.

I looked at how I may have created this karma. I saw that I had spent earlier lifetimes abusing power. One lifetime I ran a sweatshop, making young boys work beyond their capacity. I also spent lifetimes suppressing others as a slave master.

As I work out all of the fears, frustrations, and worries from these past lives, I become more and more focused on the career that is

As I work out all of the fears, frustrations, and worries from these past lives, I become more and more focused on the career that is right for me.

right for me. My finances are improving, and the business I started is supporting me and my family nicely while I'm making good progress with an even bigger dream.

WE'RE ACTORS IN A NEW PLAY EVERY TIME WE REINCARNATE

Letting go of all the pain we have experienced and caused may be difficult at first. Having a new image may help. One image we can choose is that we are all actors, each lifetime in a different play.

When we feel like victims, it's time to look at the other roles we've played. I know this isn't easy. It took me years to face the fact that I may not have been so nice in my former lives. I had to accept the possibility that I played the role of someone who caused pain or grief to others.

> As long as we learn from the roles we've played and don't accept them as our true identity, we can maintain the viewpoint of being Soul.

This is something we've all done at one time or another. As long as we learn from the roles we've played and don't accept them as our true identity, we can maintain the viewpoint of being Soul.

What other kinds of lifetimes can limit people in their careers or finances?

Larry has an unusual example:

It's been difficult for me to break through the financial wall in this life. I have worked hard to educate myself and become savvy in the business world. Still, I have failed at many business ventures and missed good opportunities, choosing the duds every time! I felt like nothing would ever work for me.

I knew it somehow related to my upbringing.

My father has always been competitive with me. He never wanted to teach me how to do things. I had to learn on my own. There was a lot of anger and verbal abuse to add fuel to the fire. Even as an adult, my father would never acknowledge my skills, abilities, or talents. However, he raves about his sons-in-law! This seemed very unusual and created a lot of self-esteem problems for me.

I had to find out why my father and I had this kind of relationship. I knew it was affecting my career. I was willing to look into a past-life possibility, and I found myself seeing images of Africa.

My father was a tribal chieftain in that life. I was his rival for chief, even though I was still a young boy.

As I grew older, he became very wary of me, trying to keep me down with taunts and insults. I didn't care much about the position of chieftain; I was too young to be interested in such great responsibility. I was only doing my duty in preparation for it. However, his abusive tongue finally got to me, and I killed him.

I finally understood how angry he must have been about that. Now we have this karma between us, and we are in this life together to resolve it.

I have worked at forgiving myself—and forgiving him for making me the underling again in this lifetime. By recognizing the blocks in this lifetime, I realized what had occurred in a previous lifetime. And I am now moving forward in my career. The forgiveness has allowed me to release the old images of being insulted by my

By recognizing the blocks in this lifetime, I realized what had occurred in a previous lifetime. And I am now moving forward in my career.

father, in both this life and the past, and the images of my feelings of failure.

I can now be more neutral, knowing I'm a different person in this life than I was then, even if my father doesn't remember past lives or work with them. I have given myself a gift of healing the old wounds, not letting them hold me back anymore.

When there is a strained or unusual work or family relationship for no apparent reason, as Larry discovered, it's time to look at the cause. In order to grow spiritually, we take responsibility for ourselves and our actions, whether in this or a past lifetime. As Harold Klemp states:

> *Each time you move from the circle of the home to the circle of school or business, you are entering a whole new world. There you will run into people who are working out their problems. While they are working out their problems, you are also working out your own.*
>
> *This is how the Law of Karma works in everyday living. The end result is that we are to become people of love and compassion who allow other people to be themselves.*[3]

Life Works Best with "Not Too Much, Not Too Little"

In past lives we have been on both sides of many situations. It's a challenge to stay balanced in the middle, not having or being too much or too little of anything. But we're all learning!

The next story shows a finer balance gained by exploring a painful former life.

In past lives we have been on both sides of many situations. It's a challenge to stay balanced in the middle, not having or being too much or too little of anything.

Timothy noticed he has felt overly responsible in this life. He learned from exploring a past life why he felt that way.

Timothy noticed he has felt overly responsible in this life. He learned from exploring a past life why he felt that way.

*A*ll through this life I've always hated owing people money. I was very apprehensive about borrowing, even if I knew I could pay it back. If my bank account got low, I became very nervous. Even just balancing my checkbook, I'd get a knot in my solar plexus. This anxiety about finances was not instilled in me in this life, so I concluded it had to come from a previous life.

I had a past-life recall where I was living in San Francisco. Poor and on drugs, I lived in an inner part of the city, where poverty was prevalent. This area was depressed and dangerous. I borrowed money to get high again. The only kind of moneylender who would deal with someone like me was the kind that would rough someone up pretty badly if they didn't pay back the loan. When the loan shark's henchman came to collect the money and I didn't have it, he knifed me in the stomach.

It was good to know how I had developed my anxiety about money. I even felt this anxiety right where I had been knifed. Once I had this knowledge, the feelings of dread and panic about finances slowly unwound over time. I'm no longer nervous about money. I have a successful career as a computer programmer, earning a good income.

My past-life memory was validated for me when I thought about the fact that I never liked the inner city. Also, I like to keep brand-new, elegant things around me, taking my imagination far from that life of desperation and destruction.

Look from the High Viewpoint of Soul to Learn

Soul is who you truly are as a spiritual being.

How do we gain the higher viewpoint of Soul that can help us see and understand the workings of this life and the past?

Try this next exercise. It helps me find Soul's higher viewpoint every time.

> Soul is who you truly are as a spiritual being. How do we gain the higher viewpoint of Soul that can help us see and understand the workings of this life and the past?

Exploration Exercise: Soul's Eye View

Premise: You may have heard it said that when you're taking a test, you should trust your very first answer as being correct. That's true for this exercise. The first thing you think of may be from the highest viewpoint, Soul.

1. Think of a work situation or career issue that makes you feel frustrated. Sing HU, as shared on page 13, to get to the highest viewpoint as Soul.

2. For this next part, don't think too much. Just let something come to mind and trust yourself to know.

   Lightly put your attention on the frustrating situation. Ask yourself, Why? Immediately say or write the first thing you think of, whether it comes in words or images. Remember, the paper doesn't judge you.

3. Now look at those images or words, and ask God to show you the whole picture. Write whatever comes to you. You may want to draw something. See how it fits with your present frustration. It may be something from a past life.

Looking at life very directly and simply, without thinking too hard about it, can be the most uplifting, gratifying experience of all. Truth is simple. Why complicate it?

Children know this instinctively. We can learn so much from these Souls in little bodies. The next chapter takes a peek into the past-life awareness of youth.

Truth is simple. Why complicate it?

8

The Ancient Wisdom of Youth

Children have the wisdom of God and are closer to it than many people who have spent years in this world gaining all kinds of knowledge about the nature of religion. Children have it naturally.

— Harold Klemp, *The Secret of Love,*
Mahanta Transcripts, Book 14[1]

_S_ome people say little children must be closer to God. Their eyes sparkle. Their hearts are open. Freshly rested between lives, maybe they remember heaven. Sometimes they remember former lives, like Jacob did.

At four years old, Jacob was riding a bike with his mother. He was looking up, chirping happily, "Isn't that bird beautiful? I remember when I was a bird. I can't remember what kind of bird, but I sure loved to fly!"

Later, he said to his father, "I was your dad once."

Jacob surprised everyone when the dog was begging. (Animals are Soul too. If you've ever loved a pet, you know their love is just as real as any human's.) Jacob told his grandmother, "I used to do that when I was a dog."

Little Janna recalled a past life too. One day she said to her mother, who was baking, "I remember when I was the mom and you were the little girl and I made cookies for *you*."

Dr. Ian Stevenson, author of *Children Who Remember Previous Lives: A Question of Reincarnation*, has done extensive research in the area of children's past life memories. A professor of psychiatry at the University of Virginia, he has found thousands of children have had spontaneous past-life recalls. Over sixty-five detailed reports he's written have been published.[2]

It seems you can learn more about reincarnation and children by asking children!

If you ask a three- to four-year-old child what they did when they were big, you may actually get an answer about the child's previous existence. Sometimes you don't even have to ask, they just tell you, like Jacob and Janna did.

Why are children so aware of their past lives when adults are not?

Their minds have not been completely "socialized." As our past-life expert, Harold Klemp, says:

> Usually children from the age of two up to five or six remember past lives. Later they forget, simply because amnesia is also a part of the deal. When children go to school and the social consciousness starts coming in, at this point it

Why are children so aware of their past lives when adults are not? Their minds have not been completely "socialized."

has been agreed that the memory of past lives is forgotten, total amnesia. The memory is totally gone; they forget everything.

This way, Soul begins with a clean slate. It doesn't harbor grudges from before. It doesn't fall into the old rut of wasting a life with unnecessary problems that belonged to last time, like getting into a duel.[3]

A CHILD'S PURE LOVE CAN HELP US HEAL

Eileen received a great spiritual awareness from one simple statement made by her small niece, Molly. Molly's mother was explaining the concept of a grandmother to her three year old. "I'm your mommy and Nana is my mommy," her mother said. Then three-year-old Molly said, "I'm her mommy," pointing at Nana. Had Molly reincarnated from a lifetime as her own great-grandmother? Eileen wondered.

At that time, Eileen's father had just died. She knew she would miss him very much. Inspired by her niece's statement, she thought maybe she would find her father in a new body. She said:

It's hard to see the connection between the person you loved and the person they may become. I know Soul is the true essence, not the role and personality. Looking for my dad to come back, I realized I might not recognize him. I started thinking, *How will I recognize him? What if I don't? He could be anyone!*

I decided I would have to love everyone! This realization really broadened my outlook on life and Soul, accepting others and recognizing the oneness of all life. Little Molly showed me a

Looking for my dad to come back, I realized I might not recognize him. I started thinking, *How will I recognize him? What if I don't? He could be anyone!* I decided I would have to love everyone! This realization really broadened my outlook on life and Soul, accepting others and recognizing the oneness of all life.

more expansive view of love, helping me heal from my father's death.

Perhaps you've experienced such a healing of awareness through the power of a child's love.

Helen received a healing from a very old heartbreak simply by listening to a three-year-old spouting truth.

J was a roommate with three-year-old Alison and her mother, when her mother decided to get married. She asked if I could take care of Alison while the new couple went on their honeymoon for two weeks. I agreed, since I'd always felt an unusual closeness to this child.

As I put Alison to bed that first night alone together, she said, "I'm going to tell you a story."

This was certainly a switch. How many three-year-olds want to tell *you* a story at bedtime? She continued without waiting for me to agree. "We used to live in New York City, and there's a sign outside our window that looks like a pickle. I am brown, and I have bare feet. My name is Latasha, and you're my mommy. You left me. Why did you leave me?"

A floodgate opened inside me. I knew what she was saying was absolute truth. I remembered the lifetime I left her, and even her name, which was unusual. It was in New York City, as she had said, and I had chosen my singing career over my daughter. It was a terrible, heartbreaking choice to have to make, and I still felt the pain of it in this life.

Alison's story also explained why several months earlier she had gotten very upset when

> I knew what she was saying was absolute truth. I remembered the lifetime I left her, and even her name.

I left the house for the first time since being their roommate. Alison had run to the door as I was leaving, grabbed my leg, and yelled, "You won't come back. You won't come back!"

We had a wonderful relationship—like mother and daughter—over those next couple of weeks. It was something I had never experienced in this life, but it was completely natural. It began the healing process that led me to forgive myself, as she forgave me completely for having left her in that past life. All this, from a three-year-old!

In a few years, Alison may forget everything about her former life with Helen. As children get older, they remember less of their past lives because they have to learn to live in this society.

Perhaps you can help your children trust you with their past-life memories. Listening to what they say with respect and openness about their past lives may help them stay open and aware as an adult.

If some unusual feelings or tendencies come up in your children, you may understand better by talking to them and asking simple questions, like Do you remember when you were big? Perhaps they will be able to share more with you if you open the door for the possibility of reincarnation. Don't be surprised if they begin to tell you stories they could never have made up!

One mother believed in reincarnation, so she was open to finding the solution to her daughter's strange behavior. The daughter, Tory, now grown, tells this story.

If some unusual feelings or tendencies come up in your children, you may understand better by talking to them and asking simple questions, like Do you remember when you were big?

*M*y mother understood about past lives, so she let me hide and tried to comfort me. But she just didn't know what to do when I would push her away and say, "You're not my mother. You're not my real mother." I remember waiting for my real mother to come. I remembered my mother from my past life, and this was not her!

Because my mother is so open to all of life and let me take the time I needed to feel comfortable with her, I was able to let go of the past. As I grew older, my mother and I became very close. We remain good friends. We're more like sisters than mother and daughter!

ADULTS MAY REMEMBER PAST-LIFE RECALLS FROM THEIR CHILDHOOD

Maybe you've had some gentle breezes from the past blow through your childhood. As you read the following stories, think about unusual situations from your own childhood that may have been remembrances from former lives.

Tory, whose mother was so open (previous story), tells us about another experience.

*A*s a young child (about three or four) I was always jumping at the sound and vibration of the trucks going by on the highway next to our house. I was so frightened, I ran under the table to hide. I remember feeling there was danger all around me, and I always had to be on alert. I was not consciously seeing a past life, but I was feeling that my survival was in jeopardy.

When I was older I saw images on television and in books about World War II. I said to myself,

> Because my mother is so open to all of life and let me take the time I needed to feel comfortable with her, I was able to let go of the past.

That's where I was, I remember that. I knew that was where I'd come from in my previous life. Then it all fell into place: that's why I was the way I was. I had been half-Jewish, and I remember having to move around a lot to not be discovered. I was married to a non-Jew, and he protected me. Yet all around us Jews were taken away, and there was always the fear of being caught. My husband was with the underground movement to help Jews escape. He was discovered by the Germans and run over by a truck; he died.

It was interesting for me to note that in this life there was always a fear of being recognized, because in my former life being part-Jewish was a threat to my survival. I had to behave and look un-ethnic, in essence, hiding who I was. These experiences and perceptions convinced me that past lives are indeed very real.

As a child, Kenny remembered a pleasant lifetime. Sometimes we have rest lifetimes that help us recuperate from lifetimes of hard work or heavy emotion.

*W*hen I was a child I loved to sit on the hill in our orchard and eat figs. A wonderful feeling came over me at these times. I had romantic thoughts of hot sunny days on a hillside far away, eating grapes and figs. I even remember doing some work in the orchard in that far-away place, digging up trees with an iron bar. As an older child, I knew I was remembering a past life in Greece. It was a pleasant, restful lifetime.

As an older child, I knew I was remembering a past life in Greece. It was a pleasant, restful lifetime.

Wayne was able to stay open to his past lives throughout his childhood and teenage years. He had some dramatic memories that he could not easily forget. One of these occurred when he was young enough to be open and old enough to remember it later. This past-life memory helped him heal an old fear of the ocean.

We took a ferry as part of a family vacation when I was around six years old. As we got to the ocean, I looked out over the water and felt deep anxiety. I grabbed a pole and wouldn't let go. Someone grabbed me and tried to make me let go. I screamed and hollered; there was no way I was going to let go of that pole.

When I was about ten years old, my family started frequenting a Greek restaurant that had an immense, realistic mural painted on one wall. The first time I saw that mural, I was nearly in shock. The mural was mostly clouds, over a Greek island. What I saw, instead of clouds, was a huge tidal wave coming right at me. As I stood there, dumbfounded, I experienced feelings, smells, and sounds of the ocean threatening to destroy me and everyone else in my village. I could even hear people running and screaming. I had drowned in that life, along with my entire village.

> Each time I stood in front of this huge painting, I experienced more and more details of that past life. Even so, I actually became calmer.

No matter how many times I saw that mural, I could never see clouds, only the tidal wave. Each time I stood in front of this huge painting, I experienced more and more details of that past life. Even so, I actually became calmer.

The mural finally lost its effect on me as I healed from the fear, anxiety, and panic of that lifetime.

Over the years I became interested in scuba diving. In my dive to get my certification, I had to overcome the last of my fear of the ocean to help another diver on our team overcome hers. It completed the healing, helping me let go of my past-life drowning fears. Now I just love diving!

Wayne had another memory of past-life recall as a child.

When I was in sixth grade, my school put on some kind of long-distance race. I started slowly, at the back, with some of my friends. Suddenly something sparked inside me, and I took off like lightning. I looked ahead and ran as fast as I possibly could to catch up to the front—to win, if I could.

I just ran and ran with all my might, passing everyone. My legs became numb, and my face pale. I came in second. After such a slow start, and never having tried to win before, this was highly unusual and a great surprise to me!

This whole experience brought up past-life memories, when I used to be a runner in South America. I was a native of the mountains and ran from village to village carrying messages. I lived to run. This was the feeling that came up when I was running the race at school in this life, but I didn't know what it was until I finished the race.

Have you known a child who is exceptionally good at some sport or musical instrument? They seem to be able to utilize the basic tools of the talent with little or no former training in this life.

In my dive to get my certification, I had to over-come the last of my fear of the ocean to help another diver on our team overcome hers. It completed the healing, helping me let go of my past-life drowning fears.

Skills from previous lives may be used in this life to further a career begun in a past life, or they may simply lay a piece of the foundation for a hobby or career in this life. Darrell is a good example. I met him many years ago and was amazed at his success when he was so young. At age twenty-one, he obtained a three-million-dollar contract to create murals in a large business setting. Darrell's talent was obvious. He had even won a national art contest at age ten. He told me that others recognized his rare talent, which came naturally to him. He was able to work in the field of art, making very good money, almost immediately. I wondered if Darrell might have been one of the famous artists who died poor and never made real money on their paintings. Had he returned in this life to collect his due?

Other people are able to take advantage of their past-life training to enhance relationships in this life. Nathan now understands the images that came to him as a child, helping him further develop certain qualities that would make him an excellent leader in this life.

> *I* always wondered about my relationship with my brother. When he was born I couldn't wait for him to grow up more, so I could do things with him and we could communicate. I always led the way and was as protective as a parent would be. He looked to me for guidance, as he would a parent. I wanted to provide it, because it just felt natural. I found myself acting more and more like a parent to him.
>
> When I was in fifth grade, I had an over-

Skills from previous lives may be used in this life to further a career begun in a past life, or they may simply lay a piece of the foundation for a hobby or career in this life.

whelming feeling that my little brother was really my son! The feeling passed, and I dismissed it. But when I got to be a teenager and learned about past lives, I knew it was true. Then I tried to consciously get out of the parental role.

Because of this past-life experience, I learned at an early age to back off from situations where I may have been pushing too hard. I pushed my little brother until I realized why. Once I understood I had been his father, I was able to let go. Remembering past lives can help present relationships be more balanced.

WE'RE NEVER TOO YOUNG TO LEARN FROM PAST LIVES

At an early age, Theresa also learned lessons to improve her relationships with others.

*T*he second I met Vick, I knew him. We were only fourteen years old, yet it felt like the fit of a comfortable old shoe. Not very romantic, I know, but that was our real relationship. We were old battle-and-beer buddies from lifetimes ago. We tried dating for a while, but we were just too similar. That's when I knew we had been warriors together.

There's still a real strong connection between us, even though we are both happily married to other people. If I'm thinking about him, he'll call. We're very good friends.

With my friend Vick, I've learned it's OK to be one of the guys, even though I'm a woman this life. After all, we've all been both sexes over and over again.

Remembering past lives can help present relationships be more balanced.

Soul Is Neither Male nor Female, Only God's Love in Action

Theresa made an intriguing comment. Soul is neither male nor female and as such can, and does, switch gender from lifetime to lifetime.

Children often remember bonds of love subconsciously, running to embrace a certain aunt or uncle. Perhaps they will even hug a new acquaintance spontaneously, feeling already connected.

A great friendship developed from a past-life connection like this. The following story is from Shawna, who is a teenager now.

I met a girl in honor band while I was attending elementary school. This girl did not go to my school, but we became best friends after just one conversation!

We have very different personalities, so no one can understand why we're friends except me. I know we were brother and sister in a past life.

A Whole Family of Friends Can Come Our Way at Any Time

Have you ever met a family with whom you felt really close?

Sometimes people feel closer to families unrelated to them. It may be confusing for youth or anyone unfamiliar with reincarnation.

Tammy found a whole family of friends in a surprising way, at quite a young age. She is seventeen years old now. As a fifteen-year-old, she traveled to France as an exchange student and had a beautiful past-life recall related to her health.

I 've always had a really strong interest in France. I was even born on one of France's national holidays, July 14. I've always had an inexplicable desire to learn French. I really love speaking it. The images I see of France in a past life are those of being around very friendly people. I had a good life there.

Even though I was in France for only one month as an exchange student, I felt extremely close to my exchange family. We just clicked. We write to each other almost once a week. This is highly unusual for former exchange students, who usually don't keep in touch with their exchange families at all!

The connection I remember with that family was in medieval times in Europe. The image I see is of someone wearing a long cloth hairpiece, like nurses would wear. She was ministering to a back injury I had from falling off my horse.

The mother in the French family in this life was the nurse in that life. The fascinating thing about my short visit with her in this life was that I injured my back again! And again, she took care of me very lovingly.

The exact opposite experience of Tammy's happened to Collette.

Although she was born in France, Collette was not comfortable there, even when she was very young. She remembers this feeling clearly, but also a specific incident which indicated an attachment to another country from a past life.

Although she was born in France, Collette was not comfortable there, even when she was very young. She remembers this feeling clearly, but also a specific incident which indicated an attachment to another country from a past life.

$\mathcal{W}$hen I was ten years old I felt I was not a French person. I began to feel that France was not my country. I could not say why, only that I did not belong in France, though it was the only place I had ever lived or even visited.

Later, at age thirteen or fourteen, I wrote an essay in school that surprised even me. I stated in the essay that my parents were not my parents and that I was from Hungary. The headmaster called my mother and asked if this was true, because it was so unlike me to do this.

I was beginning to remember my past so strongly that I had to write about it, yet I did not know why or what it was. I didn't know about past lives then.

Now, as an adult and spiritual student, I can see I was recalling my life as a gypsy in Hungary. Many pieces of my life point to it. As a child I was very fascinated with gypsies and with stories of winter and snow. Anything about snow attracted me. Even now, that is so. This past-life recall opened my eyes to the possibility that I had lived before, that I was more than just this body.

UNPLEASANT LIFETIMES MAY BE CAUSING YOUR CHILD'S NIGHTMARES

We come into
each life to
learn more
spiritual
lessons and
work out
more karma.

We come into each life to learn more spiritual lessons and work out more karma. The karma doesn't wait until we are older. It begins right away. Dreams are one way children, or adults, may work out karma from past lives.

Sometimes children have nightmares about unpleasant past lives. They may be reviewing these traumatic lifetimes in their dreams in order to learn the lessons needed. If a child is disturbed by night-mares, here is a simple exercise to help them.

Exploration Exercise: Singing HU for Help

1. Tell your child you know a way they can ask God for help before sleep, during a nightmare, or if they wake up from a nightmare and still feel scared.

2. Explain that there is a word, *HU* (explained fully on page 13), that is a love song to God and will bring God's love and protection. Your child can sing HU every night before sleep and even in dreams.

3. This word can be sung while awake as well as any time the child feels afraid.

   This exercise is so simple, it may seem like it would not be effective, but it is extremely so. It's helped children, and adults as well, to feel safer and even face their fears.

Tell your child you know a way they can ask God for help before sleep, during a nightmare, or if they wake up from a night-mare and still feel scared.

One family I know has sung HU ever since their children were born. The parents would sing HU with the children at night before bed. It helped the children overcome fears of all kinds, including past-life fears that surfaced, like with Tristen, who is in college now.

When I did a spiritual exercise to explore my fear of speaking, I saw a very clear image that was frightening because it was so real. To ease my fear, I sang HU, as I'd been taught since I was very young. Then I could observe and not be pulled into the image. Here's the past-life I saw:

I remembered being a monk during the Spanish Inquisition. I was very open minded and had ideas that were a little different than what the Spanish authorities wanted people to believe at the time. I was not trying to make other people believe what I believed, but I was very open about sharing my ideas, passing the word along to others. I just wanted to help people, but I was captured and tortured for my beliefs, mostly for sharing them. I was put in a dungeon and tortured for what seemed like months. Eventually they dragged me up to a large room to get more information from me about my friends. I told them where they were and asked to not suffer anymore. I thought the Inquisitors would then let me go. Instead they killed me. That lifetime created a fear of speaking my mind and talking about things I believe in— especially new ideas or concepts.

> Youth often have a special connection with God. They can show us how to trust ourselves more, as they instinctively trust themselves.

Youth often have a special connection with God. They can show us how to trust ourselves more, as they instinctively trust themselves. The next chapter may help you strengthen your connection with God and trust that you already have this link, because of who you are, eternal Soul.

9

Beyond Reincarnation and Karma: The View from Eternal Soul

Soul longs to return to God. The search for God is really the search for happiness, and vice versa. There is a great loneliness that some people experience—they look for a mate; they look for health, wealth, and well-being. This is Soul's desire to return to God as it manifests in the feelings that we carry here on the physical plane. . . .

Soul's mission is to become a Co-worker with God. It is simply that and nothing more.

— Harold Klemp, *How to Find God,*
Mahanta Transcripts, Book 2[1]

Soul longs to return to God. The search for God is really the search for happiness, and vice versa.

$\mathcal{N}$ow that you have read a few stories from others' past lives and perhaps even explored the possibilities of your own, have some of your questions been answered?

You may understand better why someone with a lifetime illness must learn a hard lesson from the past, or why love can go awry even when it seems so strong. Perhaps you are more receptive to the healing that can take place from past-life explorations and have seen how to overcome old fears that stand in the way. But have you wondered what happens next?

When I was a college student, I was walking through the park one day, thinking about life and death and rebirth. I was imagining there might be a way to be released from having to be reborn again and again. I had a strong inner feeling there *was* a way, and I wondered what it might be. A few months later I found Eckankar.

YOU ARE BETTER NOW THAN YOU HAVE EVER BEEN

Eckankar taught me that the many lifetimes we've lived have brought us to the point where we are today. And we are better than ever! Once we have completed our numerous experiences, playing varied roles in life after life, we are ready to return to God as a Co-worker. Harold Klemp succinctly sums up the purpose of our existence and experience:

> *If we could walk through life without any obstacles, Soul would learn absolutely nothing. The obstacles that occur along the way are to give Soul experience; they are responsible for the purification and maturity of Soul. The experiences are necessary for Soul to become a Co-worker with God. This is Its final purpose.*[2]

Was I ready to be a Co-worker with God?

I didn't know. I only knew I wanted to begin the

Eckankar taught me that the many lifetimes we've lived have brought us to the point where we are today. And we are better than ever!

journey home to God, and do whatever it may take to get there. I discovered Eckankar and was ecstatic to find it a direct path to Self-Realization (recognition of Soul, the true self) and God-Realization (awareness of the God State and our relation to it as Soul). Eckankar has illuminated the truth for me about life, death, and Soul's journey back to God.

How do we begin this journey? It's different for everyone.

We start to wake up to who we really are with the help of old friends and messengers from God. Old friends from former lives may help direct us back to our true spiritual natures.

Robert met an old friend who helped him discover his true self when he was very young.

At sixteen years old I knew nothing of the spiritual world beyond my Jewish upbringing, nor was I interested. My main goal as a painfully shy teenager was to develop social grace. How could I meet a girl?

Spirituality wasn't part of my formula for getting over my shyness, or so I thought! I just imagined myself to be more outgoing and then made the effort to talk with more women. Soon I found myself talking with a woman who recommended a Tibetan spiritual book, as it had saved her from suicide.

Something clicked in me. I got the book. This was the beginning of the spiritual search I had no idea I was on. After reading the preface of this book, I had a very clear vision of the truth: this world is an illusion, and there is another whole plane of reality! It made perfect sense to

> Eckankar has illuminated the truth for me about life, death, and Soul's journey back to God.

me. Then and there, without reading another word, I reintegrated my entire world.

Some people study Eastern religions for years before understanding them. I know now I had already studied Eastern religions for lifetimes.

When I visited Thailand, I went to the old capital where the ruins of the temples have been left just as they were lifetimes ago. I could literally feel myself meditating there as a monk. I've always loved the Buddhist writings. They've never been a mystery to me.

Having studied all these religions in depth over lifetimes, I was ready in this life to move on. I only needed a few reminders of my past to tie up some loose ends. In this life I was ready to move out of the realm of reincarnation and karma. Then I found Eckankar and knew I was home.

Eckankar is a religion recognizing all faiths as a part of God's plan. It allows spiritual freedom for all. We have the tools to get beyond the trap of karma and move into the higher levels of heaven before we even die!

> Eckankar is a religion recognizing all faiths as a part of God's plan. It allows spiritual freedom for all.

The whole reason for living many lifetimes is to get closer to God, closer to divine love—actually becoming love. As Harold Klemp says:

> God loves, but not because we deserve it or have earned it. The reason is simply that God is love, therefore God loves. We are Soul, God's creation, and It loves us because that is Its nature. We have to recognize that we, as Soul, must one day come into the fulfillment of our spiritual being too. We, as Soul, must become love.[3]

SOUL'S FULL POTENTIAL IS WITHIN YOU

The full potential of Soul is within you. Total awareness of God's love. When Soul is fully aware, It is ready to return home to God. Its lifetimes on the wheel of karma are finished, and now It can move through the heavenly worlds as a Co-worker with God, one of God's helpers. This is the ultimate goal of Soul.

How do we gain total awareness?

By extensive experience!

How else would we learn all the lessons needed to graduate from this earth academy? A variety of challenges and tests from different cultural, social, financial, physical, mental, and emotional viewpoints rounds out Soul's education.

Each lifetime teaches us many lessons to help us develop the qualities needed to become one of God's helpers. The most important of these qualities is love. Compassion is a vital aspect of love, especially for a Co-worker with God. Compassion allows our hearts to stay open and nonjudgmental in order to really listen, to truly help another Soul along the path to God. We can do that best when we understand what they've been through. That understanding may only come from experience, as painful as it may be.

Experience helps us grow as Soul. Once we are mature as Soul, we can move beyond reincarnation and karma.

How do we move beyond reincarnation and karma?

> The full potential of Soul is within you. Total awareness of God's love.

One way is to understand the universal spiritual laws, those laws that affect each and every one of us, whether or not we are aware of them. The book by Harold Klemp *The Spiritual Laws of Life*[4] is a very thorough exploration of this subject.

Another way to lessen karma is to do everything in the name of God and do it the very best we know how. This also helps to dodge day-to-day karma as we navigate the rough waters of present-day relationships, jobs, and other potential karmic traps. When we do something in the name of God, we will know immediately if it's the best action or decision. This requires trusting ourselves to be aware, listening to the Voice of God in whatever way it comes to each of us.

Another way to lessen karma is to do everything in the name of God and do it the very best we know how.

STAYING OPEN TO THE VOICE OF GOD IS EASY!

How can we keep the channel open to hear the Voice of God?

We stay receptive to God's voice by practicing and maintaining the spiritual linkup through daily practice of the Spiritual Exercises of ECK. Eckankar's writings provide many spiritual exercises you can try. Or you can refer to the book *The Spiritual Exercises of ECK* by Harold Klemp. You've already been doing some spiritual exercises if you have tried the exploration exercises in this book. The simplest is singing the word *HU*. This word will uplift you spiritually and keep you attuned with the Voice of God. All you need do then is listen!

Doing my spiritual exercises every day is as important to me as eating. I've had days where I had to make a choice and chose to do my spiritual exercises first. No matter what is going on in my life, my spiritual exercises make it better.

Singing HU with as much love as I can, while focusing on my inner spiritual teacher, the Mahanta, is one simple exercise that I use most often. When I do this, I feel as though I'm being given a rejuvenating infusion of divine love, awareness, understanding, and inner peace. There is absolutely nothing like it in this world.

Daily spiritual exercises help me hear the Voice of God more clearly. I then know what actions, words, and decisions will take me farther from karma and closer to God. As Harold Klemp states:

> *With the spiritual exercises, you can bathe in . . . the river of divine love.*
>
> *You can bathe in it, immerse yourself in it spiritually, and be purified. You can find the purification necessary to rise into higher states of consciousness, into spiritual freedom in this lifetime.*[5]

Another means of avoiding the creation of unwanted karma is to stay as balanced as possible in our attitudes and opinions. This also helps us sail through rough karmic waters.

For example, say a woman's husband leaves her for another woman. She could become angry, bitter, and resentful. She could make everyone around her miserable too. This will increase her own misery, and the sad karmic cycle continues. Or she can look at the situation as a gift from God. The gift is not obvious immediately, but she knows it is there, inside, like a pearl, waiting to be discovered. Her

Daily spiritual exercises help me hear the Voice of God more clearly.

open attitude keeps her looking for a positive, growth-producing outcome.

LIFE IS A GIFT TO MOVE US FORWARD SPIRITUALLY

Maintaining an attitude of "life is a gift" keeps us moving forward spiritually, collecting less karma and more love. It helps to have a spiritual guide through all of life's confusion.

The Mahanta is the one true friend and guide I know of to help anyone get through lifetimes of karma quickly. This is true at any time. One hundred years from now, or one thousand, the Mahanta will always be available to guide anyone who is ready to finish their karma in this life and move on to higher levels of heaven.

The Mahanta can appear as a blue light or blue star, sometimes as a pinpoint of light. I have never experienced more divine love than I have while in his presence, whether inwardly or outwardly.

This Blue Star of God, the Mahanta, is God's messenger of love, guidance, and protection for you. In the same way the wise men were guided by a star when they traveled to Bethlehem for the birth of Jesus, the Mahanta will guide you—when you ask. If you don't see a blue light, you may have a feeling of love surrounding you or hear a wonderful sound.

While many religions mention the Light of God, few refer to the Sound. Harold Klemp says:

> *Life could not exist without either the Light or Sound of God. They show up in many different*

ways here in the material plane. They create the forms within which we move to get the spiritual experience we need to have spiritual freedom.[6]

God speaks to us outwardly and inwardly through the Light and Sound. Sometimes the Light comes brightly, as It did to Saul on the road to Damascus. Sometimes It comes softly, as a small pinpoint of light, often blue, to signify the Mahanta's presence.

The Sound of God may be heard outwardly in any sound of nature or even machinery. When you hear the sound of HU, like a hum or breeze within any other sound, you are hearing the Sound of God. God is giving us love constantly through this Sound. The many levels of heaven each have their own special sounds.

The Mahanta can guide us through the many levels of heaven while we are still alive in a physical body! He can do this for us in our dreams or waking life, if we put forth just a little effort. When we do one of the Spiritual Exercises of ECK, or when we ask for help in our dreams, the Mahanta will take us on a journey. If we remember these out-of-body travels, we are fortunate.

These spiritual experiences help us lose our fear of death. We can prove to ourselves we are eternal Soul, free from the body. Traveling in the many levels of heaven, we find there are Souls living there too, experiencing life very much as we do, but often with more awareness and love.

The Mahanta, as an inner spiritual guide, leads Soul to the heavenly worlds It needs to explore. Soul is in the karmic cycle of birth and rebirth called the

The Mahanta can guide us through the many levels of heaven while we are still alive in a physical body!

Wheel of the Eighty-Four, until the Mahanta arrives to release It.

A little known fact is that the Mahanta, as well as guiding us inwardly, is always represented here on earth, in the form of the Living ECK Master. He teaches outwardly through talks, books, and discourses available to those who wish to hear his voice of spiritual truth and freedom.

There is an unbroken line of these spiritual Masters. They were all messengers of God for their times and spiritual guides for those who studied with them or called upon them.

THE MAHANTA IS A SPIRITUAL GUIDE AND INNER FRIEND FOR ALL

The present Mahanta, the Living ECK Master is Sri Harold Klemp. "Sri" is a title of respect. Members of Eckankar do not worship him, but look to him as a friend and teacher who can show the most direct route back to God.

Some of us have already met our very best friend, the Mahanta, in a past life. Here is a story of someone who recalls the meeting:

> I'm so grateful to have found the Mahanta in this life again, because I did not appreciate who he was in a past life.
>
> In a former life I turned my back on the Mahanta because unique spiritual beliefs were not accepted at that time in history. I denied my relationship with the Mahanta because it wasn't safe to say anything about it.

There is an unbroken line of these spiritual Masters. They were all messengers of God for their times and spiritual guides for those who studied with them or called upon them.

Now I am free to express my beliefs. The Mahanta gives me more love than anyone ever could. His inner friendship and guidance is always there.

The Mahanta is here to guide Soul home to God. He will give you love, protection, and guidance whenever you ask.

If you wish to know more about how to meet the Mahanta, look in the back of this book for further information, or try the exercise at the end of this chapter. If you choose, you can still stay in the religion of your choice and learn to see more truth in it by studying Eckankar. The Mahanta does not look for followers but helps those who ask.

In addition to inner spiritual guidance, the Mahanta has the power to help you finish up your past-life karma. He can also assist you over the borders of death and into the life between lives.

What happens between lives? You may meet with other Souls with whom you have shared many lives. There will be a time to rest and recuperate before reincarnating again. The book *Journey of Souls* by Michael Newton gives an account of people who were hypnotized and reported on this mystery from subconscious memory.[7] However, the book only tells part of the story.

Upon death of the physical body, each Soul must normally meet with the Lords of Karma. They are like a board of directors, deciding the best course of action for your next life. The karma you have earned up to that point must be reviewed, and these managers make sure it happens. When you study with

> The Mahanta is here to guide Soul home to God. He will give you love, protection, and guidance whenever you ask.

the Mahanta, however, you bypass the Lords of Karma. The Mahanta looks out for your spiritual welfare and guides you to your next step in a way that is most effective for your unfoldment as Soul.

The Mahanta actually takes over the karmic management for Souls who look to him as their spiritual guide. As a member of Eckankar, you also receive outer writings via discourses by the Mahanta, the Living ECK Master that are sent in the mail to help with your spiritual unfoldment. Classes are available for those who wish to study with others and are a wonderful vehicle for moving along spiritually.

A comprehensive overview of the Eckankar spiritual program is now available in Harold Klemp's two-volume set *Your Road Map to the ECK Teachings: ECKANKAR Study Guide*, Volumes 1 and 2.[8]

You may always request help from the Mahanta, no matter what your spiritual beliefs.

YOU CAN TEST YOUR CONNECTION WITH THE MAHANTA

If you want to take another spiritual step, this next exercise may help. You may always request help from the Mahanta, no matter what your spiritual beliefs.

Here is a simple way to invite the Mahanta into your life to help you see beyond past lives, into the heavenly worlds:

Exploration Exercise:

Exploring Greater Realms of Spirit

1. Find a comfortable, quiet place to sit with your eyes closed.

2. Sing HU, the ancient love song to God (ex-

plained earlier on page 13.)

3. Ask to meet the Mahanta. If you like, ask him to guide you to your next spiritual step.

The Mahanta may appear to you as a blue light, soft or bright, small or large. It may be a blue star that you see or a light of a different color.

When you see a picture of the present-day Mahanta in his outer, physical form, you may recognize him as someone from your dreams. Or he may just look familiar and friendly to you. That's because he loves and cares for all of life.

Do this exercise as many times as you like. You can try it every day until you see some results. Watch what happens in your daily life. Look for God's guidance in your waking hours or in your dreams.

The spiritual opportunities we have at this time in history are magnificent. Every kind of information is available to us, and yet we only have so much time. How do you want to spend it?

Would you like to learn more about who you really are as Soul?

Would you like to feel more free?

Would you like to get closer to God's love?

If you wish to further yourself spiritually, there are many resources available. Eckankar has great answers to life's mysteries. You have the spiritual freedom to choose what works for you from the many ways to God. Take advantage of all the growth that life has to offer. If you are interested in the most direct, clear route back home to God, Eckankar has

If you are interested in the most direct, clear route back home to God, Eckankar has the road maps, the guidance, and the means for you.

the road maps, the guidance, and the means for you.

After all, this lifetime is the foundation for your next, in this world or beyond.

Glossary

Words set in SMALL CAPS are defined elsewhere in this glossary.

BLUE LIGHT. How the MAHANTA often appears in the inner worlds.

ECK. *EHK* The Life Force, the Holy Spirit, or Audible Life Current which sustains all life.

ECKANKAR. *EHK-ahn-kahr* Religion of the Light and Sound of God. Also known as the Ancient Science of SOUL TRAVEL. A truly spiritual religion for the individual in modern times. The teachings provide a framework for anyone to explore their own spiritual experiences. Established by Paul Twitchell, the modern-day founder, in 1965. The word means "Co-worker with God."

ECK MASTERS. Spiritual Masters who can assist and protect people in their spiritual studies and travels. The ECK Masters are from a long line of God-Realized SOULs who know the responsibility that goes with spiritual freedom.

GOD-REALIZATION. The state of God Consciousness. Complete and conscious awareness of God.

HU. *HYOO* The most ancient, secret name for God. The singing of the word *HU* is considered a love song to God. It can be sung aloud or silently to oneself.

KLEMP, HAROLD. The present MAHANTA, the LIVING ECK MASTER. SRI Harold Klemp became the Mahanta, the Living ECK Master in 1981. The spiritual name of Sri Harold Klemp is WAH Z.

LIVING ECK MASTER. The title of the spiritual leader of ECKANKAR. His duty is to lead SOULs back to God. The Living ECK Master can assist spiritual students physically as the Outer Master, in the dream state as the Dream Master, and in the spiritual worlds as the Inner Master. SRI HAROLD KLEMP became the MAHANTA, the Living ECK Master in 1981.

MAHANTA. *mah-HAHN-tah* A title to describe the highest state of God Consciousness on earth, often embodied in the LIVING ECK MASTER. He is the Living Word. An expression of the Spirit of God that is always with you.

PLANES. The levels of existence, such as the Physical, Astral, Causal, Mental, Etheric, and Soul Planes.

SELF-REALIZATION. SOUL recognition. The entering of Soul into the Soul Plane and there beholding Itself as pure Spirit. A state of seeing, knowing, and being.

THE SHARIYAT-KI-SUGMAD. *SHAH-ree-aht-kee-SOOG-mahd* The sacred scriptures of ECKANKAR. The scriptures are comprised of about twelve volumes in the spiritual worlds. The first two were transcribed from the inner PLANES by Paul Twitchell, modern-day founder of ECKANKAR.

SOUL. The True Self. The inner, most sacred part of each person. Soul exists before birth and lives on after the death of the physical body. As a spark of God, Soul can see, know, and perceive all things. It is the creative center of Its own world.

SOUL TRAVEL. The expansion of consciousness. The ability of SOUL to transcend the physical body and travel into the spiritual worlds of God. Soul Travel is taught only by the LIVING ECK MASTER. It helps people unfold spiritually and can provide proof of the existence of God and life after death.

SOUND AND LIGHT OF ECK. The Holy Spirit. The two aspects through which God appears in the lower worlds. People can experience them by looking and listening within themselves and through SOUL TRAVEL.

SPIRITUAL EXERCISES OF ECK. The daily practice of certain techniques to get us in touch with the Light and Sound of God.

SRI. *SREE* A title of spiritual respect, similar to reverend or pastor, used for those who have attained the Kingdom of God. In ECKANKAR, it is reserved for the MAHANTA, the LIVING ECK MASTER.

SUGMAD. *SOOG-mahd* A sacred name for God. Sugmad is neither masculine nor feminine; It is the source of all life.

WAH Z. *WAH zee* The spiritual name of SRI HAROLD KLEMP. It means the Secret Doctrine. It is his name in the spiritual worlds.

For more explanations of ECKANKAR terms, see *A Cosmic Sea of Words: The ECKANKAR Lexicon* by Harold Klemp.

Notes

Foreword

1. Morey Bernstein, *The Search for Bridey Murphy* (Garden City: Doubleday & Company, Inc., 1956).
2. Luke 9:8 Authorized (King James) Version.
3. John 3:13 Authorized (King James) Version.

Chapter 1. Waking Up to Past Lives

1. Harold Klemp, *The Slow Burning Love of God*, Mahanta Transcripts, Book 13, 2d ed. (Minneapolis: ECKANKAR, 1996, 1997), 96.
2. Linda C. Anderson, *35 Golden Keys to Who You Are & Why You're Here* (Minneapolis: ECKANKAR, 1997).
3. Harold Klemp, *The Drumbeat of Time,* Mahanta Transcripts, Book 10 (Minneapolis: ECKANKAR, 1995), 77.
4. Harold Klemp, *Past Lives, Dreams, and Soul Travel* (Minneapolis: ECKANKAR, 2002).
5. Harold Klemp, *The Art of Spiritual Dreaming* (Minneapolis: ECKANKAR, 1999), 72.
6. Debbie Johnson, *Dreams: Your Window to Heaven* (Minneapolis: ECKANKAR, 2002).
7. Harold Klemp, *The Spiritual Exercises of ECK,* 2d ed. (Minneapolis: ECKANKAR, 1993, 1997).
8. Klemp, *The Drumbeat of Time,* 36.

Chapter 2. Uncovering the Mysterious Past

1. Harold Klemp, *Autobiography of a Modern Prophet* (Minneapolis: ECKANKAR, 2000), 107.
2. Dick Sutphen, *Past-Life Therapy In Action* (Malibu: Valley of the Sun Publishing, 1983).
3. Morris Netherton and Nancy Shiffrin, *Past Lives Therapy* (New York: Morrow, 1978).
4. Hans Tendam, *Exploring Reincarnation,* trans. A. E. J. Wils (London: Penguin Books, 1990).
5. Bernstein, *The Search for Bridey Murphy.*

Chapter 3. Resolving Fears, Phobias, and Old Beliefs

1. Harold Klemp, *Cloak of Consciousness,* Mahanta Transcripts, Book 5 (Minneapolis: ECKANKAR, 1991), 75.
2. Klemp, Harold, *How the Inner Master Works,* Mahanta Transcripts, Book 12 (Minneapolis: ECKANKAR, 1995), 221.

Chapter 4. Meeting Your Past in Romantic Relationships

1. Harold Klemp, *The Eternal Dreamer,* Mahanta Transcripts, Book 7 (Minneapolis: ECKANKAR, 1992), 144–45.
2. Klemp, *The Slow Burning Love of God,* 90.
3. Harold Klemp, *Ask the Master,* Book 2 (Minneapolis: ECKANKAR, 1994), 84.
4. Ibid., 85.
5. Harold Klemp, *Wisdom of the Heart,* Book 2 (Minneapolis: ECKANKAR, 1999), 34.
6. Ibid., 35.
7. Ibid., 37.

Chapter 5. Healing Relationships with Family, Friends, and Coworkers

1. Klemp, *The Slow Burning Love of God,* 162–63.
2. Klemp, *The Secret of Love,* 63–64.
3. Klemp, Harold, *Wisdom of the Heart,* Book 1 (Minneapolis: ECKANKAR, 1999), 25.

Chapter 6. Past Lives, Present Health

1. Klemp, *The Drumbeat of Time,* 78.
2. Klemp, Harold, *We Come as Eagles,* Mahanta Transcripts, Book 9 (Minneapolis: ECKANKAR, 1994), 19.
3. Klemp, *Wisdom of the Heart,* Book 1, 209.

Chapter 7. Careers Under Past-Life Management

1. Klemp, *What Is Spiritual Freedom?* 23.
2. Klemp, *Autobiography of a Modern Prophet,* 107.
3. Klemp, *What Is Spiritual Freedom?* 80.

Chapter 8. The Ancient Wisdom of Youth

1. Klemp, *The Secret of Love,* 96.
2. Stevenson, Ian, *Children Who Remember Previous Lives: A Question of Reincarnation* (Virginia: University Press of Virginia, 1987).
3. Klemp, *Our Spiritual Wake-Up Calls,* 118.

Chapter 9. Beyond Reincarnation and Karma; The View from Eternal Soul

1. Klemp, Harold, *How to Find God*, Mahanta Transcripts, Book 2 (Minneapolis: ECKANKAR, 1988), 120.
2. Klemp, Harold, *The Dream Master,* Mahanta Transcripts, Book 8, 2d ed. (Minneapolis: ECKANKAR, 1993, 1997), 68.
3. Klemp, *We Come as Eagles*, 25.
4. Klemp, Harold, *The Spiritual Laws of Life* (Minneapolis: ECKANKAR, 2002).
5. Klemp, *The Slow Burning Love of God*, 238–39.
6. Klemp, *What Is Spiritual Freedom?* 164.
7. Newton, Michael, *Journey of Souls* (St. Paul, MN: Llewellyn, 1994).
8. Klemp, Harold, *Your Road Map to the ECK Teachings: ECKANKAR Study Guide,* Volumes 1 and 2 (Minneapolis: ECKANKAR, 2003).

For Further Reading and Study

Past Lives, Dreams, and Soul Travel
Harold Klemp

What if you could recall past-life lessons for advantage to-day? What if you could learn the secret knowledge of dreams to gain the wisdom of the heart? Or Soul Travel, to master the shift in consciousness needed to find peace and content-ment? To ride the waves of God's love and mercy? Let Harold Klemp, leading authority in all three fields, show you how.

This book can help you find your true purpose, greater love than you've ever known, and spiritual freedom.

How to Survive Spiritually in Our Times,
Mahanta Transcripts, Book 16
Harold Klemp

A master storyteller, Harold Klemp weaves stories, tips, and techniques into the golden fabric of his talks. They high-light the deeper truths within you, so you can apply them in your life *now*. He speaks right to Soul. It is that divine, eter-nal spark that you are. The survivor. Yet survival is only the starting point in your spiritual life. Harold Klemp also shows you how to gain in spiritual wealth. This book's a treasure.

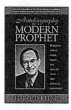

Autobiography of a Modern Prophet
Harold Klemp

Master your true destiny. Learn how this man's jour-ney to God illuminates the way for you too. Dare to explore the outer limits of the last great frontier, your spiritual worlds! The more you explore them, the sooner you come to discovering your true nature as an infinite, eternal spark of God. This book helps you get there! A good read.

Dreams: Your Window to Heaven
By Debbie Johnson

Venture in your dreams to the limits of your imagina-tion, even to the threshold of heaven. Explore your distant past, understand your present, and see future possibilities. Learn dynamic techniques and tips to mine the gold in your dreams; deal with nightmares; solve problems; review past lives; and have prophetic dreams by choice—not by chance.

Available at your local bookstore. If unavailable, call (952) 380-2222. Or write: ECKANKAR, Dept. BK49, P.O. Box 27300, Minneapolis, MN 55427 U.S.A.

There May Be an Eckankar Study Group near You

Eckankar offers a variety of local and international activities for the spiritual seeker. With hundreds of study groups worldwide, Eckankar is near you! Many areas have Eckankar centers where you can browse through the books in a quiet, unpressured environment, talk with others who share an interest in this ancient teaching, and attend beginning discussion classes on how to gain the attributes of Soul: wisdom, power, love, and freedom.

Around the world, Eckankar study groups offer special one-day or weekend seminars on the basic teachings of Eckankar. For membership information, visit the Eckankar Web site (www.eckankar.org). For the location of the Eckankar center or study group nearest you, click on "Other Eckankar Web sites" for a listing of those areas with Web sites. You're also welcome to check your phone book under **ECKANKAR**; call **(952) 380-2222, Ext. BK49;** or write **ECKANKAR, Att: Information, BK49, P.O. Box 27300, Minneapolis, MN 55427 U.S.A.**

☐ Please send me information on the nearest Eckankar center or study group in my area.

☐ Please send me more information about membership in Eckankar, which includes a twelve-month spiritual study.

Please type or print clearly

Name _____
first (given)   last (family)

Street _____ Apt. # _____

City _____ State/Prov. _____

Zip/Postal Code _____ Country _____